APPLE BLOSSOM WEEKEND

a Steve Larkin mystery

by

Dave Davis

APPLE BLOSSOM WEEKEND

© Copyright 2013 by Dave Davis

ISBN 9781490301198

2nd printing
August, 2013

1

Winchester, Virginia, 1992

This year was no different. Eddie called me at the office and told me that my annual $7 inspection sticker was going to set me back $190. According to Eddie, two tires and rear brakes were necessary to get me back on the road safely and legally. At least it wasn't as bad as last year when he hit me up for around $300. I told him to go ahead and do whatever it takes.

"When can you get to it?" I asked.

"It's done" Eddie replied. "I took the liberty."

"All right. I'll be over after I get some lunch."

Nothing was going to ruin today. Today was my favorite day of the year. It just happened to fall on Friday, May 1st, this year. I was ecstatic, not because it was the 63rd Shenandoah Apple Blossom Festival Weekend, not because it was the 118th Kentucky Derby weekend and not because it was my brother's 32nd birthday tomorrow. It was the end of finals week. Another semester, another year was over. Happy New Year!

Five dimes bought me six Lance peanut butter crackers from the mostly empty vending machine around the corner from my office. I remembered my brother telling me years ago, when we caddied together at a country club, that Lance crackers were the best. I walked down the dimly lit, empty hallway and turned my grades in to the secretary for the College of Agriculture and Forestry.

"Here you go Joyce. I'm all done."

She looked up at me. "Put it on the stack. Are you teaching summer school?"

"Hell no." I said proudly.

"Well then, you lucky bastard, have a great summer."

"I intend to."

Poor Joyce. She only gets two weeks of vacation per year. One she has to spend with the in-laws near Gatlinburg, Tennessee. The other is her family vacation to Virginia Beach in August. I don't know which would be worse.

I had a terrific job and I knew it. I was paid pretty well for a nine-month, non-tenure track, 100 % teaching appointment. I enjoy telling people that I'm knocking down five figures and then watch their reaction.

I left Pierce Hall on the east side of the building and walked alongside a solid row of Japanese yews that were old and tired. It was the last of four yellow brick buildings in a row where the campus ends and the town of Winchester begins. There isn't any overlap.

It was a cool, crisp morning that was evolving into a gorgeous afternoon. A welcome change from all the rain we had in April. This was the kind of day that car wash owners pray for and the kind of day that forces morel mushrooms to erupt from the ground.

When I jaywalked across Market Street, a horn blew and some young girl shouted: "Asshole."

I waved. She was probably a former student. I walked past the Yukon Railroad, a bar which in the six short years that I had been in town had changed its name more times than Elizabeth Taylor. I then entered Valley Newsstand and peeled back the left hand corner of the Winchester Star. Pittsburgh 9 Atlanta 3.

"Yes!" I blurted out a little too loudly.

What a day. Following the Pirates was more than a pastime for me. It was my stock market, my soap opera. It set my mood for the rest of the night or the next day. Whenever they won I would spend the quarter to read the box score. Losses were free. Mrs. Henderson, the lady behind the counter looked terribly uncomfortable sitting on her stool. She was leaning forward, resting her arms on the counter. Her head was turned ninety degrees toward the front door. She was restless as if expecting a crowd of people to rush in at any time. Perhaps she was worried the crowds might not come on her busiest weekend of the year. She had spent months ordering and stocking Apple Blossom hats, buttons, key chains, t-shirts and coffee mugs, and only had three days to move all the crap.

"Just a paper, Mrs. Henderson."

"Twenty five cents, please, Big Spender."

"Town's getting crazy." I remarked.

"Tell me about it."

She was looking through me to get to the next customer. I folded the paper and placed it in my briefcase. I was hoping the Pirates would cost me $25 in newspapers this season. Adjacent to the newsstand, I entered the Blue and Grey Café where I ordered a tuna sandwich and a large unsweetened iced tea. I ate and read the sports page for twenty relaxing minutes. The Pirates had a three game lead on the second place Mets, Eighteen horses were running in the Derby tomorrow and Ernie Irvan was on the pole for the Winston Cup race at Talladega on Sunday.

Outside, traffic was picking up. Most of the students were gone by now but the Apple Blossom Festival tourists were rapidly taking their place. Airstream trailers were running rampant. I sure was glad I wouldn't be around for the festivities. I turned the corner on Fairmont Avenue and headed north.

I could smell the apple juice plant long before I could see it. The plant bellowed steam into the air from various stacks. The season for pressing juice was coming to a close just as this year's crop was about to emerge. Thousands of empty wooden bins, stacked ten high, were waiting to be picked up and returned to orchards scattered throughout the Shenandoah Valley. I walked two blocks past the plant and entered Eddie's Garage and Video.

The garage was located north of town between the campus and the fast food Mecca just inside the bypass. Eddie had inherited the four-bay building from his grandfather, the late Henry Gardiner. Henry ran the Chevrolet dealership there for years but sometime in the 1970s he converted it into a repair garage and switched from dealing to turning wrenches.

Back in the 1950's, the dealership was a good mile out of town on the Martinsburg Pike. Now, the garage was definitely in town, partially due to the last annexation, and a pretty valuable piece of property. From the outside it looked like an antique used car lot. On the lot was a '52 International pickup, a post World War II Willys Jeep, a '66 Cadillac Sedan De Ville and a couple of Corvairs.

Inside, on the far side of the shop, was Eddie's prized possession. Parked in the fourth bay, under a car blanket, was a Tuxedo Black '68 Chevrolet Chevelle SS two-door convertible. The big 396 cubic-inch engine, largest of the V-8s, produced 325 horsepower with a four-speed manual transmission. Eddie's grandfather helped him purchase the car after high school. Eddie rarely took it out, but when he did everyone knew who was behind the wheel.

Eddie's father, Arthur Robinson, was an orchardist. When Henry retired, Art wanted nothing to do with the garage, so he gladly handed it over to Eddie. I really liked Art. Though most of the courses I teach at the college deal with

8

ornamental horticulture, I know enough about fruit tree production to relate to Art.

Eddie liked mechanic work. It was satisfying. He enjoyed diagnosing a problem and fixing it. What he didn't like was the F word.....FARMING. Eddie wanted as little to do with the orchard business as possible. He had worked on the family orchard occasionally as a teenager, but in high school he took a job filling up the rubber machines in the local men's restrooms. After high school he worked for his grandfather full time until he retired. Eventually Eddie took over the garage and changed its name.

Eddie's Garage was pretty run down. It was poorly lit and poorly insulated. Repair manuals and parts were piled on tables. Calendars with naked women were still hanging from decades long gone. A few years back, Eddie renovated part of the building into a video rental business. Customers enjoyed browsing through video boxes while waiting on their vehicle. The adult movies were hidden and had to be requested from a list in a three-ring binder.

Eddie's wife Linda, whom he calls Skull because according to him she is hard-headed, manages the video store. But since hiring her niece, Becca, to run the place, she doesn't come around much anymore. Skull was also a decent mechanic but since marrying one, she didn't mess around with it much anymore either.

When I opened the shop door, a bell clanged and a light brown and white bulldog trotted up to give me the once over. Country music was seeping out from a bookshelf. I closed the door and when I bent down to greet Rocket, he walked off.

Eddie was in his mid-thirties, 5' 10" in height but appeared taller in blue coveralls. His face was thin with a moustache that covered his upper lip and sideburns that were obsolete. His brown eyes seemed small under his bushy eyebrows. A greasy NASCAR Skoal Bandit ball cap, signed by Harry Gant, covered a full head of light brown wavy hair. He was a very talented tavern athlete. He would excel as a competitor in a pentathlon of pool, darts, foosball, shuffleboard, and pinball.

Eddie was pacing behind the counter holding a cordless phone with two greasy fingers. Occasionally he spit in the direction of a Maxwell House coffee can on the floor. He yelled at the phone.

"I wouldn't even own a car with three goddamn brake lights."

As he caught a glimpse of me he pulled the phone away from his left ear. Then he pointed at the phone while looking up in the air. He brought the phone back to his ear and listened for a few more seconds. He yelled again.

"Fix it? Yeah I'll fix it. I'll rip the son of a bitch clean out of the car. Then all your brake lights will work."

Eddie listened for a few more seconds and then said, "Okay. Can you bring it in next week? I'm heading out of town this afternoon."

Eddie put the phone down on a Chilton's parts manual and turned to me.

"Steve, Ol' buddy. You after that Bronco?

"How'd you know? You in a bad mood?" I asked.

"Christ, it's been a rough week. Everybody's bitchin' about something. I'm waiting on a bunch of parts and my racing fuel order is two days overdue. It's always crazy the week of apple blossom."

I moved a box of piston rings and placed my briefcase on the table closest to the antique cash register. I popped open the briefcase and wrote out a check for $190.

"I didn't know you sold racing fuel."

Eddie hesitated as if he wasn't sure if he sold it or not and then looked at me and said "I sell a little. I have some regular customers."

I changed the subject and asked "Are you ready to get out of town?"

"I've been ready. Skull is still pissed at me from last weekend."

"What happened?" I asked pretending to be interested.

"I went turkey hunting on our anniversary."

I gave him The Look.

"It was the last day of the season.... I didn't know I'd be out there all day." Eddie said, trying to justify it.

"Hey, speaking of Skull, did I just see her drive off?"

"Yeah. She just left."

"She got a new vehicle?" I asked.

"Yeah. She got another Blazer."

"What was wrong with the other one? It wasn't that old."

"Hell if I know." Eddie said shaking his head. "I think she said it rode too rough. I wasn't listenin'. Anyway, she traded the four-wheel drive one in for an older two-wheel drive. It's a 1988 model."

"Are you sure you don't want to stay and watch the parade tomorrow?" I asked jokingly.

"Yeah, I'm sure." Eddie said. "Even a bad day of fishing beats eating funnel cakes and watching Joan Rivers, Jerry Mathers or some other asshole ride through town."

"No, man. This year the Grand Marshall is Willard Scott. " 'How do I know that?', I thought to myself.

Eddie's four favorite things to do in order were: fish, drink, screw and sleep. That phrase might make a great tee shirt design.

"Where do you want to go?" I asked.

"When do you have to be back? Eddie asked.

I thought for a little while and said, "Labor Day." He didn't get it.

11

"Well, we can fish the Silver for a while or we can just go straight to the cabin and fish Back Creek," Eddie said. "I was just up there yesterday."

"Let's go to the cabin and stay a couple nights." I suggested.

What Eddie called the cabin was actually an old house on the western edge of the family orchard. It was a white two-story stick-built house situated about fifty yards from Back Creek. It used to house migrant workers, but with the reduction in acreage, and thus workers, the house had become vacant. Eddie talked his dad into letting him convert it into a cabin/retreat.

The Silver River didn't have much personality. It was homogenous, lacked cover for the fish and didn't have much current. There was very little riparia and the bank had been eroded, in many areas, from cattle. It had a lot of fishing pressure since it flowed beside Route 608. It got hammered with worms and Power Bait but it was stocked weekly and drew a lot of fishermen like Eddie.

Back Creek, on the other hand, was a decent trout stream that flowed northeast and eventually spilled into the Potomac River. It was shady and fed by several springs that kept it cool enough for, mostly brown trout, to carry over through the hot summer months. It was also stocked in several places. But the little less than one-mile section that flowed through the orchard property was posted.

"Let's go to Back Creek." I said. "How soon can you leave?"

"As soon as Luis gets here. He's going to cover for me and close up this afternoon. Evidently he didn't show up for work today at the orchard. Which is unusual. Anyway, he called and said he had to go check something out in town and then he'd be over. We're closed the rest of the weekend."

Luis was one of six Mexicans left working on the orchard and also a pretty good mechanic. Pioneer Orchards actually came from Eddie's mother's side of the family and in 1956, Arthur married into 600 acres of high quality fruit production. Eddie's mom, Catherine, was an only child and so was Eddie. Eddie was born in late September, 1958, smack dab in the middle of the Red Delicious harvest season.

"I'll pick you up around 3:30." Eddie said. "I got a tape I want you to hear."

Eddie was into country music in a big way. He liked everything from Marty Robbins to Marty Stuart. He was definitely country when country wasn't cool. Hell, Winchester had a country music tradition and line-dancing had recently become the latest craze. One of Eddie's uncles, on his father's side, claimed to have gone out with Patsy Cline a few times. He also claimed she was a slut.

I enjoy almost every kind of music except main-stream country. Alabama and Garth Brooks just didn't do it for me. Polkas I can live without and I enjoy reggae for 45 minutes or one song, whichever comes first. I grew up with Steely Dan, Tom Waits, Jim Croce and The Guess Who. The closest thing to country music that I listened to in college was southern rock. My brother used to claim that the best country band around was Creedence Clearwater Revival.

But that had all changed after I met Eddie. Whenever we go fishing, we take turns playing music and try to convince each other that what we like is awesome. Eddie picked up the phone on the second ring.

"Racing fuel hotline." He said proudly. He listened for a couple of seconds.

"I got a little left but it's going fast. Get here before 3:00. I'm closing early."

The bell rang as I left the shop and climbed into my Bronco. When I fired it up, the wipers came on, the fan was on high and of course country music blasted out of the radio. Without thinking, I punched the station selector before turning down the volume.

After returning the dashboard to normal, I caught Eddie in my rearview mirror, smiling through the shop's front window. I also noticed the Trout Unlimited sticker on the back glass of my Bronco and it reminded me of how

Eddie and I had become friends four years ago. The first time I had him do an inspection he noticed the sticker and we ended up talking about fishing for over an hour. Since that day we have fished together many times in Virginia and West Virginia.

I pulled the gear selector into drive and tested my new brakes while easing off the lot. I struggled to come up with the best bootleg route back to my house. It was less than two miles the way the crow flies, but the crows had left town for the week-end.

2

You can tell a great deal about the personality of a neighborhood by the size of the houses, the vehicles in the driveway, the landscaping and by the brand of beer can that you find in your yard. The houses in my neighborhood were built as single family homes. But now that the university had grown so much, many had been cut up into apartments. I parallel parked, with ease, walked around the Bronco and picked up a Milwaukee's Best can in my front yard.

I had rented 229 Park St. since moving to Winchester in 1988. The two-story brick home was built in the 1930s and was fairly small on a tiny lot. The adjacent houses were very similar and within spitting distance of my front porch. The rent was reasonable and the place was pretty quiet for being so close to campus. I had yet to find a Heineken bottle in my yard.

Mrs. Cochran, next door, was sitting on her porch peering around the left side of her newspaper.

"Are you drinking beer already?" She asked when she saw me with the bottle.

"No. Not yet." I smiled and kept walking.

"I am." She yelled back.

I opened the mailbox and removed a Sears's flyer. Under it was a Publishers Clearing House Sweepstakes envelope informing me that I might already be a winner. I entered the house through the front door, which incidentally few people do anymore, and glanced at the answering machine. The light was not blinking.

It was a pretty typical bachelor pad. I had the minimal amount of furniture needed and few posters decorated the walls. There were no animals to let out, no fish to feed, only a few plants to care for. After taking a serious look at the treadmill, I said "Nah, not today."

I spent another twenty relaxing minutes reading the rest of the paper. After checking my watch, I decided I'd better get my act together. It wouldn't take long to pack though. I fish so often I never really unpack.

I gathered up some trout flies that I had tied in late March. Now that it was May, and the water had come down considerably, I wanted to try some dry flies. I opened my dry fly box and added some Adamses, Blue Duns, Royal Wulffs and Mr. Rapidans. I put some homemade leaders in my vest and grabbed some cassettes. I owned a few compact discs but none of Eddie's vehicles were equipped with a CD player. After two trips to the front porch, I was raring to go. I still had some time to kill but Eddie was usually early, especially when fishing was involved. I thought about shaving but quickly talked myself out of it.

I heard a horn blow three times, so I switched on the porch light and locked the door behind me.

"You ready?" Eddie yelled.

"Ready." I confirmed.

"Luis never showed up so I just closed up early."

I threw my crap in his Suburban and jumped in. The radio was tuned to Q102, Winchester's most popular country crap station. Eddie turned toward me.

"I like your plan," he said. " Let's save the Silver for another day. I reckon it'll be pretty crowded with all the people in the area and being a Friday and all. But right now I need to run by the house for a few minutes."

Eddie lived west of town, which was on the way, off of Route 632 but everyone out there called it Nichols Creek Grade. He and Skull built a brick rancher on four acres in the early 80s to get away from the family orchard.

In its heyday, Pioneer Orchards produced mostly apples on approximately 600 acres. A few acres were devoted to peaches and cherries. Today less than 250 acres were still in production. Over the years, spring frosts, drought and poor prices had taken their toll on the apple industry in the area. Several blocks of trees had been abandoned or were converted to corn or hay. Now the majority of the fruit is sold to the processing plants for juice or sauce while only a small percentage is retailed at the roadside stand. Art was hoping prices would improve this year. Eddie was hoping the housing industry would continue to thrive.

For years Winchester's growth had marched westward into orchard country like a Civil War battle. Housing subdivisions were aggressively replacing blocks of trees. Since both demanded high ground, there wasn't much compromise. Eddie was hoping the front line would soon make it to Pioneer Orchards. Though he would never tell his father, he was ready to sell out. He had already thought of names for streets at Pioneer Heights. Easy St., Fast Lane and Jackass Court were among his favorites.

We weaved down Park Street passing piles of crap in the street and on the sidewalk that the students had thrown out. There were chairs, rugs, TVs, and bookshelves. Eddie turned right onto Valley Avenue and then quickly darted into the left turn lane and pulled an illegal U-turn. After about a mile, Valley Avenue became one lane. In the north bound lanes there must have been a hundred fire trucks lined up for the Fireman's Parade that evening. They came from towns like Clearbrook, Strasburg, Whitehall, Gore and Wardensville. When I was a kid, all fire trucks were red, now some are yellow. Finally we were able to turn right onto Nichols Creek Grade and headed west. At this point, most of the traffic was heading into town.

Eddie's little development was called Cedar Orchard which irritated the hell out of him. A couple years ago we had a good laugh trying to figure out how the development might have been named. Cedar trees aren't grown in orchards and in fact, the eastern cedar is actually a juniper (*Juniperus virginiana*). They grow wild on crappy soils and are sometimes called the poor man's Christmas tree. Furthermore, they host a fungal disease called cedar apple rust. When cedar trees grow near apple orchards, the disease can infect the apple leaves and fruit. So we concluded that some ignorant, dumbass developer pulled two words out of a hat and paired up the words cedar and orchard to name the development.

Eddie pulled into the half-circle driveway. I jumped out to soak up some sun while Eddie ran into the house. It faced the east and most of the lot was behind it. Three vehicles occupied a good chunk of the side yard and three dogs tied to individual black locust trees watched my every move. The vehicles were barely antiques and not quite worthy of being parked at Eddie's Garage and Video. Parked very close together were a Camaro and two Vegas. Eddie sprung out of the kitchen door with his gear and cooler.

We both jumped in the Suburban and Eddie took off while I was trying to figure out the seatbelt. We continued down Nichols Creek Grade for three miles and turned right on Route 621.

"How's your father doing?" I asked as I shoved a Lyle Lovett tape into the player.

"Ah, he's okay. The frost season's almost over. He's got a pretty good crop so far, so he's been in a pretty good mood."

Six miles later we rolled into the little unincorporated town of Fenwick and Eddie pulled into Bullis's Grocery.

"I need a few things." Eddie said.

"What are we doing for dinner?" I asked.

"There's stuff at the cabin. I put some deer tenderloin in the freezer yesterday."

We entered the store and headed straight for the beer cooler. Eddie grabbed a 12 pack of Schaefer for $5.30 and I picked up 6 Molsons for $5.90. The lady behind the counter was sunk in her chair and waited until the last minute to get up.

"Will that be all?" She asked.

Eddie said. "Give me a can of Skoal, a bag of ice, and let me have one of them new lottery tickets."

Eddie paid and walked outside. When I got back to the Suburban, I noticed he had removed some worms from his cooler to make room for beer.

"You're not going to use worms this time of year are you?" I yelled at him.

"If I have to I will."

I had been trying to lure Eddie away from bait fishing for some time. I had tried to explain to him numerous times the satisfaction one feels when catching a fish on a fly you've tied yourself. In return he would explain to me what great satisfaction he gets out of catching fish on night crawlers he had caught himself in the backyard with a flashlight and a coffee can.

We continued heading west on Route 621 at a pretty good clip. Eddie ejected my tape after the song "She's No Lady, She's My Wife" ended. He replaced it with Travis Tritt. Eddie sang along with Travis:

There was a time, I could drink my cares away
And drown out all of the heartaches that hurt me night and day.
When the thought of you came crashing through, I'd have one more
But now the whiskey ain't workin anymore.

Eddie took a long slug off his can of Schaefer. We veered right on Route 627 and headed northwest for about ten minutes. Finally we came to a stop sign on Route 652. A left turn was a steep uphill grade for three miles that led to the Wild and Wonderful West Virginia state line. We turned right.

After two miles of winding slightly downhill, we reached Back Creek. The stream was the western border of the most westerly block of Pioneer Orchards. Eddie stopped on the bridge and we checked out the stream.

"Looks good!" We both said at the same time.

Eddie immediately turned left after the bridge and passed his own 'Posted, No Fishing' sign. Back Creek was stocked upstream from the bridge where there was access. From here, the road turned to gravel and followed the stream. Eddie drove slowly, avoiding several large but shallow holes in the road holding water from the recent rains. Immediately to the right was a pumpkin patch that would be planted in June long after the last chance of frost was gone. Off in the distance to the right, and up the hill, was a forty-five-year-old block of Stayman apples. Their distinctive sweet-tart flavor, crispness and crimson color made them a local favorite since their discovery in 1866. They were not very popular outside the Commonwealth. It reminded me of New Englander's love for McIntosh.

We drove by the spray shed. It was a square white wooden building with stairs leading up to a landing that was about a half story tall. From there the sprayer could be filled from a pipe that was fed by a well. Inside the building were bags of fungicide that control diseases such as scab, sooty blotch and cedar apple rust, insecticides that control insects such as rosy apple aphids, leafrollers, leaf hoppers and codling moths, and herbicides that burn down thistle, nutsedge, and Johnson grass. The empty pesticide bags were burned in a 55 gallon drum outside.

Next we passed a pole barn that housed two Massey Ferguson tractors, a John Bean air blast sprayer, and a bush hog. In the corners were piles of tractor parts and old batteries and tires.

The last building was a small cinder block shop with two bays. Benches with greasy tops ran around the inside perimeter. It was heated with apple wood by a wood stove. The SevenUp soda machine provided the only light at night.

After the shop, the road rose slightly for a quarter of a mile and ended at the cabin. It was a good seventy-five feet above the stream which you could still see, but barely. This higher ground was rocky and there were several large tulip poplar trees shading the cabin. Eddie parked and we jumped out and met behind the vehicle.

"What do you want to do?" I asked.

"Let's fish.... Let me grab a couple beers and put the cooler on the porch."

Eddie returned and lowered the tailgate and the two of us wrestled on our waders and boots. Eddie put his worms and two beers in his fanny pack and grabbed his ultra-light Ugly Stick rod. I assembled my 9-foot, six-weight, Sage fly rod.

After getting our shit together, we walked around the right side of the cabin and got on the trail that led down to the stream. I led the way.

As we walked I noticed the redbud flowers were fading, but the dogwoods and cherries still provided patches of white in the otherwise green woods. Tent caterpillars had set up shop in some of the cherry trees. May apple plants were up and new fern leaves were expanding. I walked through a spider web and tried frantically to pull it off my face. I cussed and wondered why a frickin spider would spin a web six feet off the ground anyway.

I stepped off the trail, pushed my waders down with my left thumb just enough to take a leak and pissed all over a cluster of Virginia bluebells. I hadn't seen a snake yet this year and didn't want to start today. "What are you going to use?" I inquired.

"I'm thinkin' a Rooster Tail or maybe a Panther Martin," Eddie said quickly.

"Good," I said. "Save your garden hackle for the Silver."

Eddie wasn't interested in what I might use. I figured he would use spinners for maybe a half hour and then switch to worms or Power Bait.

We continued down the trail. The sun was filtering through the sugar maples and tulip trees. We came to a clearing and I looked downstream and something caught my eye. I stopped suddenly and Eddie walked right into me.

About 50 feet below us, a girl was lying on the rocks facing the sun. Her feet were in the water and she was mostly topless.

"Look." I whispered. "Some chick is laying out."

It was silly to whisper. She wouldn't be able to hear me over the sound of the stream rushing around and spilling over rocks.

"What should we do?" I whispered.

"I don't know about you, but I'm going to check her out" Eddie said in a normal voice.

Eddie passed me. We walked ever so slowly trying to get a good look before we startled her. Eventually we got within 20 feet of her. She had a medium build, very tan and long almost black hair. The water on her breasts was beaded up like they had been Turtle waxed. She must be cold, I thought.

Eddie walked a little closer, stopped and yelled. "Hey! ... Hey! ... Yo!"

She didn't respond. Eddie walked closer and kept trying to get her attention. I suddenly froze when I figured it out. Eddie was now almost over top of her. Then he turned and looked at me in horror. He had figured it out too. As my good friend R. Satterfield would say: "She was deader than four o'clock." I looked at my watch. It was 5:45.

Eddie stooped beside her and moved her face side to side. His face looked shocked and puzzled at the same time. He would look at her, then look down like he was trying to figure something out and then gaze at her again.

I bent down and took my first good look at her. She was Mexican. Not some local hairy pit, vegetarian, braless sunbather. Not some student from campus working on her tan before she had to report to her meaningless summer job at the city pool.

She was wearing jeans and red Keds sneakers. Her yellow blouse was unbuttoned and pulled halfway over her arms. A gold cross on a gold chain hung from her neck. There was a gash on her right temple and her head had swollen. I had never been this close to a dead body.

Eddie finally said. "God Dammit. Look at her. Son of a bitch."

He was getting angrier by the minute and in deep thought.

"What do you think happened to her" I asked.

"Looks to me like some bastard hit her up side the head with a rock."

"Do you know her?" I asked.

Eddie hesitated. "No.... Not really. She's Luis's girlfriend. She cleans the garage for me every other week or so."

"What should we do?" I said.

Eddie didn't say anything for what seemed like a long time. "Well, I'll go find a phone and call the sheriff. There's no phone in the cabin or the shop."

"Oh fuck! The last thing the sheriff will want to do this weekend is investigate a dead body."

Eddie knew the sheriff a little and a few of his deputies. They patronized his shop and bowled against Eddie's team.

"What about calling 911?" I said.

"Nah. Shit, they'll send five EMS vehicles and ten frickin deputies out here."

For a brief moment, I imagined all 100 fire trucks from town racing out here; after the parade of course.

Eddie looked at me and said, "All right. You stay here. I'll probably have to meet them by the bridge or somewhere, I don't know. They'll never find this place. It might be an hour or so till I'm back."

"Should I cover her up?" I asked.

"I wouldn't." He said. "Just leave her."

Eddie picked up his rod and fanny pack and scurried up the trail. I sat on a rock and took turns staring at the stream and the dead girl for what seemed like an hour. By now it was nearing 7 o'clock and the sun was threatening to move behind the sycamores that lined the other side of the stream.

A few bluish grey mayflies began emerging from the surface of the water. They appeared to be of the *Paraleptophlebia adoptive* species. They were molting from the larval stage into adults. Once an adult, they only live for one or two days. Just long enough to mate. They were dancing on the water. Tonight they were full of life.

I looked back at the motionless girl. There would be no more dancing or mating for her.

And then, somewhere near the middle of the stream, I heard a big splash. My head jerked around and I saw a wave of ripples. There was one less fly on the river.

All right! I scanned the stream with my eyes and ears. Then, there was another splash, this time along the far bank. And then another. My eyes grew wider and my heart started racing. The hatch was on and the uninvited trout were crashing the Friday night dance.

"What the hell? What else am I going do?" I thought to myself.

I looked back at the body of the girl. She was lifeless, among all this commotion going on in the river. I convinced myself that she would want me to fish. Life must go on, at least for a day or two.

I thought to myself, it would suck to be a mayfly and be devoured by a trout before you had sex. The best way to go would be

to emerge on top of the river, early in the morning, and stretch out your newly developed wings for the first time. Then fly above the river chasing some hot fly releasing her pheromone while playing hard to get. Eventually nail her in mid air while she wraps all six of her legs around you. Then fly higher and enjoy the afternoon sun before returning to the river as a worn out spinner in the early evening. Hell, I probably wouldn't mind being eaten after all that.

I fumbled around in my vest searching for my dry fly box. Fish continued to rise. I removed the nymph from my tippet and replaced it with a size 14 Blue Dun Parachute. I stood up, pulled the waders out of my crotch, and cautiously stepped into the stream. I made several good casts upstream to a pool behind a rock. On each cast, the fly drifted for five or six seconds before the current pulled it under.

"Come on.... Come on.... Hit it," I said, trying to encourage the trout to choose my fly, the only artificial fly on the river.

I decided to cast straight across the current toward the far bank where it was pretty shady. I took a few more steps in to deeper water to make room for a longer back cast. Several casts landed near the bank that had a good long drift. Fish were taking flies, but not mine.

By now there were hundreds of flies in the air and on the water. The fish were taking advantage of the show. I heard a big splash behind me where I had just been. I turned around and saw flies swirling above the girl on the bank. The sun was starting to set on her too.

I cupped my hand, bent down, and scooped up a fly off the water. It was clumsy and staggered around on the palm of my hand like it didn't have a care in the world. Perhaps it had just had sex.

Then it occurred to me that my fly was too large. I clipped it off and replaced it with a size 16, the smallest one I had on me. I made a quick short cast. I sure was glad that I tied these Blue Duns as a parachute because the white hackle above the wings stuck out in the crowd amongst all the other flies.

I decided to cast downstream for the first time. I pulled the line up off the water and made a false cast several feet downstream toward two medium sized rocks. In my back cast, I let about two more feet of line slip through my left hand to add distance to the next forward cast.

Just then I realized the fly couldn't be more than three or four feet above the girl on the bank.

"Christ. What are you doing?" I said to myself. I might have some explaining to do if the coroner found a fly in her scalp.

I panicked a little, rushed the forward cast and fucked it up. The fly hit my rod and a pile of line lay in front of me. I cussed myself, regrouped quickly and made some false casts a little farther upstream. I cast forward, let the line go and the fly actually landed one foot behind the rock I aimed for.

Crunch! My fly disappeared and the line went taut. The fish dove and hunkered down behind the rock. Then, without warning, it shot out of the water twisting back and forth. Water sprayed from the fish like a shaking wet dog. It smacked the water four feet behind the rock and headed to the bottom. It was a nice fish and it hunkered down again. I kept the line tight but didn't pull too hard. It turned into a waiting game. We were both trying to feel each other out. What would he try next? I hoped he wasn't planning to make a run for it upstream toward the log in the river.

After twenty long seconds, the line tension increased. I let out some line while he slowly worked his way down to the end of the pool. Just when I thought he was tiring, he shot back upstream passed the rock and jumped into the next pool. I pulled a little harder than I intended to--I was nervous. If I pulled too hard he might break the line, but if the line wasn't tight enough he might make it to the log.

It was a nice fish. I pulled in line while slowly wading upstream. I wanted to hold it and ask it why it chose my fly. I had plans for this fish. It was getting darker and I couldn't see the bottom of the river any longer.

"Where the hell is Eddie?" I wondered. "Don't leave me out here all night."

I had no flashlight, no vehicle and the cabin surely was locked. Perhaps I would keep this fish and eat it raw while I waited for Eddie, as Santiago had to do in Hemingway's *The Old Man and the Sea.*

I reached the rock, pushed off of it and stepped up into the pool. By now, there was only fifteen feet of line between the two of us. I pulled him in slowly. A very nice brown trout. I reached down to pick him up. He took a good look at me and must have uttered vamoose. He jerked to the right, rolled over, broke the fly off and was gone.

"Son of a bitch." I yelled. "Can you believe that?"

"Where the hell is Eddie?" I was ready to vamoose too.

3

Just as I was about to bushwhack it out of there, I heard some men coming down the trail. I quickly turned and became relieved to see several flashlights. I could hear the men singing. A Garth Brooks song I think.

'What the hell?' I thought to myself.

Six men emerged from the woods. Eddie led the way followed by four county deputies and some guy in a white lab coat who works for the coroner. They were fired up and feeling no pain. One deputy walked over to the stream and dropped his flashlight while pissing. Eddie walked up to me, no longer wearing his waders, and rolled his eyes.

"What took you so long?" I whispered.

"It took a lot longer than I thought to round these guys up. I only know two of them. Oh, and evidently the real coroner had too good a time at the annual Stag Lunch this afternoon. He's unavailable."

The coroner wannabe kneeled down by the body and took her vitals. I looked over at Eddie and he rolled his eyes again. He ran his flashlight up and down her body, hesitating at her breasts a little longer than necessary.

"There must have been some sort of struggle." He blurted out.

Eddie said softly to me, "You think, Quincy, M.D.?"

As my good friend R. Satterfield would say: "This guy didn't know his ass from page 8."

After about ten minutes of examination, they painstakingly placed her on a stretcher.

"Eddie, you ready to go?" asked the deputy with the smallest belly.

"We're going to hang out for awhile." Eddie said. "You guys go ahead. Can I keep this light? I'll check in with you tomorrow."

"Okay. You two aren't leaving town are you? I think I'm supposed to ask that." Another deputy asked.

"Nah. We'll be around."

We watched them stumble up the hill until their lights eventually disappeared.

"What do you make of that?" I asked shaking my head.

"Any weekend other than this one." Eddie fired back.

"What do you think happened?" I asked.

"They've been partying all day. Ain't it obvious?"

"No.... No, I mean to the girl?"

"Shit if I know. Why her? Why here? What was she doing here?" Eddie kept asking himself.

Eddie was pacing, scratching his head. I couldn't see his face well but I could tell he was getting worked up. He was trying to put two and two together.

"What do I care anyway? Eddie blurted out. "I could care less."

"I couldn't care less." I said.

"Why could you care less?" Eddie asked puzzled.

"I don't. What you mean is you couldn't care less." I said.

My father was an English professor and he has corrected my grammar and usage for as long as I can remember. He retired recently but still continues to correct me or will explain the origin and meaning of a particular word or phrase when I return home for a visit.

For instance, if I were to use the expression "butt naked," Dad might interject something like: "The standard expression is 'buck naked,' and the contemporary 'butt naked' is an error that will get you laughed at in some circles. Originally a 'buck' was a pretentious, overdressed show-off of a man, condescendingly applied in the US to Native Americans and black slaves, so the word 'buck' quickly acquired negative connotations. To the historically aware speaker, 'buck naked' conjures up stereotypical images of naked savages or--worse--slaves laboring naked on plantations. Consider using the alternative expression 'stark naked'."

Or, he might say, "It's Crackerjack. Not Crackerjacks."

Eddie gave me a strange look and said "Let's get the hell out of here."
"Sounds good to me. Let me get my rod."
I started reeling in my line when Eddie figured out that I had been fishing. Normally he would have complained that I got to fish more than he did but right now he had too much on his mind to be a wiseass. He mumbled something to me but all I could make out was the word *bastard*.

We walked up the trail as quickly as we could with gear and only one flashlight. Neither one of us was in the mood for small talk. When we arrived at Eddie's vehicle, we were both a little winded. Eddie opened the rear door of the Suburban. While I was removing my waders, Eddie was more interested in what was in the cooler on the porch. He returned with a beer, popped the top and took a long slug.

"Where's mine?" I asked.

"Sorry. Let's go in the cabin and get something to eat."

I agreed. My crackers and sandwich had worn off a couple of hours ago. Eddie fumbled with the keys in the dark. When he leaned on the door, it swung open.

"Shit. The door is open." Eddie said surprised.

He switched on the kitchen light just inside the front door. I hadn't been inside since last fall and the odor of the place hadn't changed.

Eddie set his beer on the counter and his cooler on the floor. The dark brown paneling kept the cabin pretty dark, especially at night. I walked into the dining room and switched on the light. Much to my surprise, the table had been overturned along with the dry sink. The drawers of an antique desk had been emptied. The dish cabinet had been knocked over and the floor was covered with broken ceramic plates and bowls. The chairs had been smashed except for one sitting upright in the corner. On the chair was a note and under the chair was a wristwatch. It was a man's watch with an expensive gold frame, and the crystal was broken. Without thinking, I stuck the watch in my jacket pocket and yelled for Eddie.

"Get in here."

Eddie walked in with his beer to his lips but quickly noticed the damage.

"What the fuck?" He yelled.

"Look." I said, pointing at the note.

Eddie pushed me out of the way. He looked down and read the note printed in large letters.

Tu Seras el Siguiente.

Eddie's eyes grew wide.

"What does it say?" I asked.

"It says You're Next.... Which means.... I'm Next."

4

We looked at each other and made a bee line for the kitchen. Eddie grabbed the cooler and headed toward the door. I turned the lights off behind us. We shot out of there faster than gasoline through a funnel and eggs through a hen. We jumped in the Suburban and all eight cylinders screamed to life. Eddie made no attempt to avoid the rain-filled holes in the road. At the end of his road, we turned left instead of crossing the bridge and heading back toward his place. After about four miles and a seemingly eternity of silence, we arrived at the intersection on Route 522.

Eddie turned to me and said. "Let's go back to town. I need a drink."

We turned south and after a couple miles, merged onto Route 37, the half-circle bypass around the west side of town. At the first exit, we got off and turned east onto Route 50, heading right back toward the mess we had left town to avoid. As we stopped at the red light across from the hospital entrance, Eddie was pounding the steering wheel and mumbling. The light turned green but Eddie just sat there staring into the distance.

"You're up!" I blurted out.

He came back to reality, floored it, shot across the intersection, ran up on the berm and demolished a group of political signs bunched together before coming to an abrupt stop. We ran over Re-Elect Robert Wilkins - Sheriff, Elect Bill Clinton President, Vote For James "Jimmy" Smith, Assessor, Judy Carlisle For City Council, Re-Elect Bush & Quayle, Frank Wolf For Congress and Ross Perot–Reform Party. We destroyed Democrats, Republicans and neutral school board members.

"What the hell's wrong with you?" I demanded.

"It's Lily."

"Who?"

"Liliana!.....The dead girl." He hesitated. "I've been messin around with her for a couple years."

"Really?" I asked.

"Yeah. I know I told you I didn't know her well. But between me and you, I know her a lot better than I'm supposed to."

"Shit. We better get out of here before somebody sees us," I said.

Eddie floored it and swerved back on the road but not before running down a Vote YES For Frederick County School Levy sign. After a mile he turned right onto Shenandoah Boulevard and pulled into the parking lot of the first bar we came to, Patricks Pub.

"This ok?" Eddie asked.

"Sure. You need to get out of this vehicle."

We got out but it took a while to reach the door. Eddie kept looking behind him, as if someone was following us, and I was gazing at the sky. The stars were out and the temperature was dropping quickly.

Patricks Pub was a unique place. It drew locals from town and employees from the juice plant, mostly for lunch and happy hour. It was also close enough to campus to draw students on party nights which was most every night. However, nothing about Patricks resembled a Pub. It had no British memorabilia, no flags, no dart boards, no rugby or softball team photos, no trophies and no Guinness posters. It had more TVs than beers on tap. Face it, it was a sports bar. Neither one of us frequented the place often and tonight I didn't know what to expect.

It was busy but not packed. Two young girls sitting near the door were sipping on their Zimas. One girl looked frightened and I heard her say in horror to her friend, "I, like, have to go to, like, summer school and take, like, chemistry. The middle-aged lady playing pinball was dressed as if she could have been married to Gomez Adams. Eddie and I sat down on the only two empty bar stools adjacent to each other.

MC Hammer's song, "U Can't Touch This" was pushing its way through the smoke-filled room. I spun my stool around and stared at Mrs. Adams's backside. I was pretty sure I wouldn't be able to touch that either. As my good friend R. Satterfield would say: "I'm hornier than a three-peckered poodle."

Pool balls were cracking in the next room. The guy beside me was drinking a High Life and looked like a carnival worker. He was about 28 years old, skinny, dirty, had a five-day beard and a Rebel Flag bandana on his head. The guy beside Eddie was much older and was wearing the official Apple Blossom Festival garb, green pants, a pink shirt and yellow tie. He was spiffy.

I was interested in two of the TVs. One was showing the baseball highlights for the day. The Pirates were losing to the Astros. The other TV was tuned to a local network showing highlights from the Fireman's Parade. If anybody's house, within a one-hundred mile radius, caught on fire today, they might be shit out of luck.

The bartender finally discovered us, blew her smoke up in the air and headed our way. As I often do when seeing a woman for the first time, I checked out her face, then her breasts, glanced at her left hand hoping for a bare ring finger and returned to the breasts. She was five feet, ten inches tall and her dark brown hair was graying. She wore jeans, a tight black sweater and had a very nice body for a gal in her early 50s. But her face was wrinkled and I could read between the lines. It was obvious she had been around the block a few times.

Eddie waved his arm and ordered. "Sweetheart, give me a can of Busch and a shot of Beam."

She looked at me, half-heartedly smiled, and said "You?" I checked out the taps.

"I'll have a Lowenbrau draught, the adult size, and some mozzarella sticks."

She nodded as if she okayed my order and walked off. Eddie walked over to the pay phone and deposited some coins. I watched him intensely. I was hoping his mannerism might reveal some clue as to what had happened. I was pretty sure Eddie hadn't told me everything he knew. The telephone cord was short, but he paced back and forth as much as he could. It reminded me of a dog chasing after something in the yard and running out of chain. After maybe ten rings, he hung up. I looked over at the guy sitting next to me.

"What do you do?"

"I work for the carnival.... Well, I did."

"Did?" I asked.

"Yeah. I've been operating the Tilt-A-Whirl for about a year. Then, last month they moved me up to The Scrambler. That's my favorite. That ride takes a little more skill to run. Anyway, I was having a bad day today and then about three hours ago, some kid spit on me. Well, let me tell you, I says I don't need this crap and just walked off. I ended up here."

He took a big slug from his bottle of High Life. "Screw it. I could care less! And as far as I know, that little bastard is still going around in circles."

"You mean you couldn't care less."

"What?"

"Never mind."

Our beers showed up and I said. "Get Scrambler here a Miller on me."

"Thanks man."

We toasted to the carnival and I took a big swallow.

I looked at Scrambler and said, "If Miller is the champagne of beers, then Andre must be the beer of champagnes."

"What?"

"Nothing."

Eddie had returned and was talking to the guy beside him. I nudged him in the side. "What are you two talking about?"

"He's a lawyer and he's pretty drunk. He asked me if I need an attorney and gave me his card. I told him not yet, but it's early."

Sweetheart returned and leaned on the bar in front of me.

"Having a good day?" I asked her.

"Yeah. Not bad. It's been pretty quiet for Apple Blossom.... A couple of rowdy drunks.... Some kids ran out on their tab.... Usual stuff. The big news is some girl was killed out in the county this morning."

"Really?" I said.

That got Eddie's attention.

"Yeah. You didn't hear? They keep interrupting the highlights of the parade. Some guy in here earlier said she was raped and beaten up pretty bad."

"That's terrible." I said, shaking my head.

She leaned a little closer toward me, looked me in the eye, and said, "She was just some Mexican!"

Well, you should have seen Eddie. He jumped up, threw down a $10 bill and started for the door. He stopped in his tracks, turned back around and grabbed the attorney's business card. He latched on to me by the collar and pulled me off the stool.

"We're out of here."

"My mozzarella sticks." I yelled as he dragged me toward the door.

5

There is an old saying in Winchester. "There are two kinds of people in town: those who own the apples and those who pick the apples."

The tree fruit industry in Virginia was well underway by the turn of the 19th century and by 1814, Thomas Jefferson had planted over one thousand fruit trees in the South Orchard at Monticello. And though orchards can be found throughout The Commonwealth, the greatest concentration lies in the upper Shenandoah Valley.

Perhaps the most prominent family responsible for the growth and wealth of the tree fruit industry in the valley were the offspring of Richard and Evelyn Byrd. They had three children: Tom, Dick, and Harry--in reverse order.

Harry Flood Byrd, perhaps Richard's favorite son, was born in 1887 in Martinsburg, W. Va. and began leasing his first apple orchards near Winchester at the age of nineteen. He bought his first orchard six years later in 1912. He later entered politics and was elected Governor of Virginia in 1926. Next he served in the United States Senate from 1933 until 1965, longer than any other Virginian. By the 1950's , Harry F. Byrd Sr. and his three sons — Harry, Jr., B. Beverley Sr., and Richard Sr., owned 6,000 acres of orchards that spread from Charles Town, WV, to New Market, VA. The operation known as H. F. Byrd

Inc., produced two million bushels of apples per year and included a cannery and packing houses. Harry Sr. was one of the world's largest individual growers--and a millionaire.

The apple business was his first love and he never left it; he was always there at harvest time, picking apples and supervising operations. First and foremost, it was a business to him. He applied to it the principles of hard work, attention to detail and adoption of new marketing techniques that he had embraced as a young newspaperman. But he was also a farmer, knowledgeable about his crop and its production; he was an innovative, nationally known orchardist, using the most up-to-date scientific methods of spraying and fertilizing, while introducing new varieties of apples to the area. Harry also hosted an annual Fourth of July picnic for his workers and families.

Dick Byrd, was born Richard Evelyn Byrd, Jr., in Winchester in 1888. He was named for his father and proved to be the most adventurous son. He was educated at the Virginia Military Institute, the University of Virginia, and the United States Naval Academy. He was attached to the naval aviation service and was placed In charge of navigation preparation for the first successful Trans-Atlantic flight in 1919. He directed the Navy unit for MacMillan's Arctic Expedition in 1926.

His greatest achievement was as commander of an expedition to Antarctica. The expedition returned safely to America after having made many discoveries of importance. He was the first man to fly over both the north and south poles and was awarded the Congressional Medal of Honor. Thus Rear Admiral Richard E. Byrd upheld the family tradition of courage and leadership manifest in the Byrds in America.

Thomas Bolling Byrd was born in 1889. He was also brilliant and likeable, but did not seek the fame that came to his brothers. In 1920, he left his law practice in Richmond, and moved to Berryville, Va., to become a partner in the family's apple business. He later relocated to Rockingham County, in the central Shenandoah Valley, and planted several orchards. He and his brother Harry changed the name of their operation to H. F. and T. B. Byrd.

The majority of the tree fruits grown in the Shenandoah Valley are apples. The apple harvest season lasts approximately nine weeks and which runs from Labor Day through the first week of November. Securing a dependable labor force to harvest the fruit for a mere nine weeks has become more and more difficult every decade since the early 1900's.

Harvesting apples is very hard work. Picking-bags are strapped onto pickers' backs and can weigh 40 lbs. when full. Long, cumbersome ladders must be moved around the orchard and used to harvest the tops of the trees. September afternoons can be quite hot while late October mornings can be frosty. Pickers are paid by the bushel or bin and must hustle to make a decent day's pay. Heavy rains can delay harvest or cause it to come to a halt for several days. Idle pickers are unpaid and unhappy.

By the middle of the 20th century, more and more locals became unwilling to pick fruit. As the local harvest crews began to dry up, growers searched for alternative labor. Mexicans, Jamaicans and Central American workers came on the scene and were willing to work. These migrant workers brought new challenges to the industry. Aside from the language barrier, labor camps had to be built to house workers and meals had to be prepared. Most workers were illegal and often crews were rounded up and deported at the worst possible time.

By the 1980s, more and more Hispanic workers became legalized, gave up migrant work and settled down in various towns. Some still worked on orchards but many found more steady work in restaurants, construction, and the landscaping industry. Today, small orchards can usually scrape up enough labor for the harvest season but many larger operations now hire off-shore pickers through a federal government program.

Each community has accepted the onslaught of Hispanic people and their culture at their own pace. Some have been slow to welcome and adapt to their new citizens. I believe the Byrd family would have welcomed the modern orchard workforce with open, harvesting arms.

6

"Stupid bitch." Eddie yelled in the well lit parking lot.

He picked up a rock and winged it at the bar. It made a loud cracking noise as it bounced off the siding.

"Forget her man. Let's get out of here." I said.

While Eddie was in the back seat grabbing a couple beers out of the cooler, I took out my Leatherman tool and cut several wild chicory shoots growing up through the chain link fence. Chicory, a member of the Aster family, is a herbaceous perennial plant. It produces sparse bright blue flowers and is actually quite pretty for a wildflower/weed. The root is used as a coffee additive and is popular in the southern U. S., especially in New Orleans. Dad said his parents tried drinking it during World War II, but they didn't like it.

Eddie popped open a can of Schaefer, turned to me and said "Blivs?"

"Sure. Let's head downtown."

We turned south on Shenandoah Boulevard which merged into Berkeley Avenue soon after we crossed the railroad tracks. Eddie parked in the only available spot and when I got out, the door bumped a fire hydrant.

"Nice spot." I said.

"I know," Eddie said. "I've parked here before. Don't forget your flowers."

"I got 'em."

The street and sidewalks were littered with cotton candy sticks, popped balloons, and silly string from the Fireman's Parade. Several people were staggering about. Some girl with pigtails was getting a piggy-back ride. She had a twelve pack of beer in one hand and the other was swirling her sweatshirt around like a lasso. "Giddy Up!" She ordered. "I'm gonna ride you all night."

Eddie looked over his shoulder as we made the turn onto Piccadilly Street. Several blocks ahead we could see the lights from the carnival. We walked two blocks and entered O'Blivions, our favorite bar in town. The place was hopping but mostly with strangers. Many hermits and old hippies converge on Winchester only during Apple Blossom weekend. You never see them the other fifty-one weeks of the year.

Four bluegrassy looking dudes were in the corner picking an instrumental song. "Foggy Mountain Breakdown," I think. O'Blivions hosts the Tuesday Night Dart League and a coupla years back I joined Eddie's team. Since then, the place has really grown on me and has become my favorite hangout in town.

Judd was perched on a stool, working the door checking IDs. He was a regular that helped out the owner on special occasions. Judd was a tall, thin guy who looked much older than he really was. As my good friend R. Satterfield would say: "His graying hair made him look extinguished." We weaved our way through the crowd waving to some familiar faces.

Our beers, along with a spit cup for Eddie, arrived at the bar before we did.

"Hey guys!" Kelly was excited to see us.

Kelly was a real cutie. She had long red wavy hair, and tonight wore green shorts and an Apple Blossom T-shirt from the 80s. She's originally from the D.C. area. Though not the brightest bartender in town, her good looks and bubbly personality made up for it. She'll say things like "I killed that bird with two stones." However, she somehow finished her degree in marketing but just couldn't bring herself to cross back over the beltway for a decent job. She had become what's known as "A Townie."

Being a horticulturist, I enjoy giving plants away, especially flowers. I help myself to some from the college greenhouse, I find some in the woods, and I steal some from neighborhoods that I walk through. However, I'm pretty good as a pruner and know how to take a cutting without leaving a hole in a flower garden or shrub.

"These are for you." I handed Kelly the bouquet and she became even more excited. "Yay! I was hoping you would bring me something. What are they?

"It's *Cichorium intybus*."

"Come again?"

"Chicory." They aren't fragrant but she wasted her time finding that out.

" Pretty blue! I'll get some water."

She walked off and I looked over at Eddie.

"We used to call those crotch keys." I said, chuckling.

"You planning to get a key to Kelly's crotch?" Eddie asked.

"Nah. I'm just a nice guy."

I kept an eye on the TV in the corner. I was hoping to catch the final score of the Pirates game, but for the time being, I had to watch highlights from the Kentucky Oaks race earlier in the day from Louisville. The "Oaks," as local residents simply refer to it, and the Derby are the oldest continuously contested sporting events in U. S. history, and the only horse races to be held at their original sites.

The first running of the Kentucky Oaks was on May 19, 1875, when Churchill Downs was known as the Louisville Jockey Club. The race was founded by Meriwether Lewis Clark, Jr. (an offspring of William Clark who went to the Pacific Coast and back to Missouri with Meriwether Lewis). The race covers 1⅛ miles and the horses carry a maximum 121 pounds. The winner now earns a $600,000 purse and a large garland of lilies, affectionately called the "Lillies for the Fillies."

Attendance at the Kentucky Oaks ranks third in the continent trailing only the Kentucky Derby and the Preakness Stakes. The Oaks, the Black-Eyed Susan Stakes, and the Acorn Stakes are the counterparts to the Triple Crown of Thoroughbred Racing, held at Churchill Downs, Pimlico Race Course and Belmont Park, respectively. Today's Oaks' winner was "Luv Me Luv Me Knot," ridden by Fabio Arguello.

Suddenly some girl slid in between Eddie and me and grabbed both of us by the ass. "Hi, fellas. Having fun yet?" She said.

"Well hello there." I said.

She let go of me, turned toward Eddie and kissed him on the cheek.

"Oh, Hi, Jenny. Good to see you." Eddie said.

"Don't be a stranger." She whispered and walked off.

"Who was that?" I wanted to know as we both watched her walk away.

"Jenny Mills. I've known her since high school. She's been after me for years."

"Man, what a body." I said.

"I know. Believe me, I've thought about it, but so far I've kept my distance. Her husband is twice my size and a very jealous person. He's threatened me before."

We both took a long slug off of our beers. I glanced back at the TV and got the bad news. The Astros had whipped up on the Pirates 10-4 in Houston. Fortunately, the Mets also lost to the Cubs earlier in the day at Wrigley Field.

"Hey, there's a board open." Eddie yelled in a surprised voice.

Kelly returned with her chicory shoots in a beer pitcher, and since we weren't carrying our darts, I asked her for the heaviest set of bar darts. We walked over to lane 1, set our beers down and I started assembling the flights on the shafts.

Eddie grabbed his stomach, looked down, and let out a long deep burp.

"Whew! That was almost a fart! It could have gone either way."

Eddie took a long swallow from his beer and said. "I'll be right back. I gotta make a call."

Less than a minute later he returned, looking puzzled.

"What's the matter?"

"It's Skull. She's still not home."

"Should she be?"

"Hell, I don't know. Let's throw a game. It'll take my mind off of things. What'll it be?"

Eddie was a terrific 501 player. I was better at Cricket. Last fall, after a horrific 501 game, I went home and wrote a song about darts. The chorus ends with:

> Don't need a nine mark,
> Don't need a ton.
> Why can't I hit that
> Frickin double one.

I chose 501 even though I preferred Cricket. Eddie needed to relax and darts just might do the trick. We both threw pretty well for our first game, but after seven throws each, Eddie had a slight lead. It was his turn and he had 91 left. I stared at the 17 and sure enough he hit a triple to leave him a 40 out. His second dart was too high and sailed over the double 20 wire. Eddie took careful aim with his last dart but before he could release it, suddenly a dart came out of nowhere and landed near the bullseye.

"What the hell?" Eddie demanded.

He turned around to find a pistol pointed up at his temple. The gunman was maybe five-feet, six inches tall and the members of his gang were all two to three inches shorter. Eddie was surrounded. Someone screamed behind me but I didn't turn around. Eddie turned slowly toward the gunman.

"Nice shot Luis. But we're not playing a doubles match. Do you want the winner?"

"Cut the shit Eddie. Why'd you kill her?"

"I didn't kill anybody."

"What was she doing at the cabin?" Luis demanded.

"I don't know. I really don't know." Eddie yelled.

"She said she was meeting you last night."

"I never met her," Eddie insisted. "I was bowling last night."

"She got a call, around 5:30. Said she had to meet you later at the shop."

"I called her to come clean the place. You know she cleans for me every couple weeks. I never met her though. I told you. I was at the bowling alley."

Eddie was getting through to him and Luis lowered the pistol.

Eddie faced him and said "Why did you leave me that note?"

"What note?"

"In the cabin. You know. *Tu Seras el Siguiente.*"

"Man, I didn't write no note."

Sometime during the heated argument, the band stopped playing and everyone quieted down. Three cops arrived and handcuffed Luis while his Mexican entourage skedaddled. Eddie tried to convince the cops to let Luis go but they insisted on running him in for brandishing a weapon. As the cops led him away, the place erupted with cheers. People were raising their drinks high in the air and patting the cops on the back. The band broke into "He's In The Jailhouse Now."

Eddie stabbed his dart into the table and chugged his beer down. He looked at me.

"Did that just really happen?

"Sure did. You were cool though. Do you want the winner? You crazy bastard, he could have popped you."

Kelly ran up with two more beers. "Are you guys ok?"

"Yeah. It's cool!" Eddie assured her.

"Well that's the most exciting thing that's happened in here today. Earlier some guy was choking on his Doritos. I thought I was going to have to perform the Heineken maneuver on him."

Eddie and I looked at each other.

"Thanks Kelly. Here take this." I handed her ten bucks. "Keep it."

"Now what?" Eddie asked.

"What are you thinkin'?

"I'm thinkin' about heading north."

"Really?"

"Heading North" was Eddie's code words for going to the strip club. When Patsy Cline started out, she had to cross over the border into West Virginia to sing. She was too young to sing in the Virginia clubs. Today, in Winchester, if you want to go to the titty bar, you have to leave The Commonwealth and go to West By God Virginia. It was about a twenty minute jaunt up Route 11.

"You up for it?" Eddie asked.

"Well, Ol' buddy, I think I've had enough excitement for one day."

"You leaving?"

"Yeah. I think so."

"You want a ride?"

"Nope. The walk will do me some good."

We finished our beers and returned our mugs and darts. On the TV was a weather alert. Widespread frost was forecast for most of the valley. I spruced up the chicory in the beer pitcher and waved so long to Kelly. A couple guys stopped us and patted Eddie on the back while we tried to leave.

"Way to go man. You stood up to those pricks."

Eddie just nodded. Judd saw us coming and stood up.

"Sorry bout that, Eddie. Those wetbacks just blew right past me. Luckily I found some cops outside."

Eddie cringed. "Yeah. It's my lucky day."

7

We stepped out onto Piccadilly Street and Eddie leaned on the double set of parking meters with both forearms. I rolled the collar up on my jacket to keep the cold air off my neck.

"You sure you want to head north?" I asked.

"Hell, I don't know. I don't feel like going home."

"You better watch your ass. Those amigos might be out there waiting for you."

"I doubt it. They'll wait for Luis before trying anything."

"Well, come on then. Let's have a couple nightcaps. I'll stay out for awhile longer. Hell, It's Apple Blossom.... Besides, maybe the Snow White Grill is still open."

We trotted across the street and turned right on Loudoun Street which has been a vital marketplace for more than 250 years. About 20 years ago Loudoun Street was closed to vehicle traffic and converted to a pedestrian mall which is now known as "Old Town." The buildings are made from brick and limestone with chimneys and wooden shutters. Since Apple Blossom Mall opened in 1982 and along with various strip malls scattered around the outskirts of town, Old Town has had to reinvent itself.

Old Town hosts art galleries, antique stores, boutiques, an ice cream parlor, outdoor cafes, fun and specialty retail shops, a couple of bars and a hardware store with hardwood floors. There is no Hardrock Café to be found.

It also contains some historic attractions such as Stonewall Jackson's Headquarters Museum and George Washington's Office Museum. A one-block section is a designated year-round Farmer's Market. The buildings downtown are really cool and can easily make one drift back in time. Tonight I was pretty buzzed and reminiscing about what Winchester was like way back in time.

Though little is known of specific tribal movements prior to European contact, the Shenandoah Valley was a sacred, common, Indian hunting ground. By the 17th century the valley was thought to have been controlled mostly by the local Iraquoi. By the time European settlers arrived around 1729, the Shawnee were the principal occupants in the Winchester area.

Quakers and Germans settled in Winchester in the early 1700s. By 1738 these settlements became known as Frederick Town. George Washington spent a good portion of his young life in Winchester helping survey the Fairfax land grant for Thomas Fairfax, Sixth Lord of Fairfax. During the French and Indian War, General Edward Braddock's march to Fort Duquesne crossed through this area in 1755. Knowing the area well from work as a surveyor, George Washington accompanied Braddock as his aide.

In 1756, on land granted by James Wood, Colonel George Washington designed and began constructing Fort Loudoun, which ultimately covered one acre in present-day downtown Winchester on North Loudoun Street. Fort Loudoun was occupied and manned with guns until the start of the Revolutionary War. At the age of 26, Colonel George Washington was elected to represent Frederick County to the House of Burgesses.

During the Revolutionary War, the Virginia House of Burgesses chose local resident and French and Indian War veteran Daniel Morgan to raise a company of militia to support General George Washington's efforts during the Siege of Boston. He led the 96 men of "Morgan's Sharpshooters" from Winchester on July 14, 1775, and marched to Boston in 21 days.

During the war, Hessian soldiers were known to walk to the high ridge north and west of town, where they could purchase and eat apple pies made by the Quakers. The ridge became known as Apple Pie Ridge.

Of all the history in this quaint small town, the Civil War is by far the most intriguing. Winchester was a key strategic position for the Confederate Army during the war. It was an important strategic area for 'Stonewall Jackson's defense of the Shenandoah Valley in 1861, Jackson's Valley Campaign of 1862, the Gettysburg Campaign of 1863, and the Valley Campaigns of 1864. Historians claim that Winchester changed hands as many as 72 times during the war. Both Union General Sheridan and Confederate General Stonewall Jackson located their headquarters just one block apart from one another at various times during the war.

"Steveo." Eddie yelled. "Are you drinkin or you going to stare up at the sky and walk around in circles all night long?"

I collected myself and reentered the 20th century. The Snow White Grill was closed but we were standing directly across the street from The Crystal Bar. The Crystal was downtown Winchester's dive bar. It was pretty cool though. The student bars can get pretty old pretty quick, so a visit to a good old fashioned dive bar can really be refreshing. Occasionally when I've had a rough day or just feeling a little down on myself, a trip to the Crystal will usually cheer me up. I come out of there realizing my life ain't so bad after all.

The Crystal is decorated in a western theme. The ceiling is nearly twenty feet high with deer antlers mounted high on the dark brown, knotty pine paneled walls. Below the antlers, bras hang from retired beer taps. The piano in the corner never gets used, compared to the pool table that gets used continuously. Out back, an outdoor patio area is equipped with a bar and grill. The Men's room has a urinal that almost wraps around you.

The bar was built locally and made from local rough-cut white oak. It runs up the right side of the front room. Behind the bar, obscure and profound bumper stickers cover most of the glass on the beer coolers. Eat Berthas Mussels; My Bartender Can Beat Up Your Therapist; Go Skins!; If You Don't Like My Driving, Stay Off The Sidewalk; and, of course, Virginia Is For Lovers, to name a few. Along with the usual stuff, the coolers were stocked with some unusual western beers such as: Olympia, Lucky Lager, Rainier and Anchor Steam.

While crossing the street, two teenagers on skateboards nearly ran us over. One of them yelled, "Hey, it's Elvis."

We came to The Crystal's front door just as some guy was sneaking out with a can of Schaefer beer. Eddie stopped him.

"You leave any Schaefer for us pal? Eddie blurted out.

He looked at us like we were the Gestapo. "Yeah, they have plenty."

Eddie turned around and yelled out the door at him. "They better!" He turned to me and said, " I love their slogan."

"What slogan?"

"Schaefer's slogan: The One Beer To Have When You're Having More Than One."

Eddie looked at me and said, "Hey Elvis, you might want to put your collar down."

Dwight Yoakum had control of the jukebox for the time being. We squeezed into a spot at the bar. Eddie got Ronnie's attention pretty quickly and ordered and paid for two Schaefers. He left one behind and walked off toward the back. I tried to keep an eye on him but he disappeared in the crowd.

I took a slug off of my beer and came close to spitting it out. "Wow! That's worse than I remember," I thought to myself. My stomach was grumbling. And as my good friend R. Satterfield would say: "I'm so hungry I could eat the balls off a low flying duck."

I looked at the guy to my left and realized he was in a deep conversation with me. He wore a white long-sleeve shirt with a black vest and a black bowler hat. He reminded me of John Hartford, the famous banjo player. However, this guy was pretty drunk and slurring his words. He tapped me on my arm every time he tried to make a point.

"...they're not gonna do nothing about it. Those bastards.... There ain't nobody there to monitor it. They'll just do it again.... And what do they care if they get fined? They can afford it. Know what I mean? Those jack asses probably paid somebody off. But, what they don't know is I'm gonna monitor it myself. Know what I mean? I'll take samples and get 'em analyzed. They don't know who they're messin with...."

I nodded a few times pretending to be interested. I turned to the gal on my right. She was a mess. She looked like she just returned from a three day caving trip and just as drunk. She grabbed my right arm with both hands.

"... I don't know where we went wrong...," she said. "I reckon we got hitched too young. It was his idea though...Now look at him. Look at her...She was a tramp in high school. You hear me? ...Ever since I went to night shift I knew something was up. Anyway, it's over. You hear me? ...I threw most of his crap in the dumpster this morning.... Oh shit! What the hell is he gonna wear to the parade tomorrow?"

Oh my God! I thought to myself. What have I gotten myself into? I slowly turned to my left, and sure enough....

"...all those sons-a-bitches care about is making a buck.... When I get my license back, I'm goin out there. I'll show 'em.... I'm bringing 'em down, baby!"

I turned to my right. Miss spelunker was sobbing.

"...her hips gave out on her early. She was only eight years old. You hear me? She was just a puppy when I got her. The vet wanted $1,200 to fix her so I had to put her down. I didn't want her to suffer no more. Hear me?"

I stared straight ahead and wished I had blinders on like the horses will wear in the Derby tomorrow. Miraculously the bartender showed up.

"Hey buddy. You got a phone call."

"Really? Who could that be?"

"Yeah. It's down there."

Without having to think twice, I abandoned my Schaefer and backed away from the bar. I walked to the end where the bartender was waiting for me.

"Where's the phone?"

"There's no call, man."

"What?"

"You looked like you needed rescued. I figured you put in enough community service for one night, listening to those two drunks."

"Thanks man. That was bizarre.....I owe you."

Eddie showed up beside me with a Busch Light and a mixed drink.

"Where have you been?" I asked. "And what's that?"

"Mint Julep. The official drink of the Derby! I've been outside on the deck. I've been talkin to the undercover ABC guys. They hate it when I recognize

57

them. One of them has a fake handlebar mustache tonight. Those guys are a hoot."

Eddie swallowed half of his drink.

"Hey, get this. The mayor is back there and his ride in the parade tomorrow fell through. So he asked me if I would escort him in the parade."

"What did you tell him?"

"I told him we could ride in the Chevelle. I haven't driven anyone in the parade for three or four years."

"Who've you been hanging out with?" Eddie wanted to know.

"You wouldn't believe it. I can't even describe it. See those two people over there? They wore me out. OK, man, I'm taking off. I'll get my gear out of your vehicle tomorrow. Hey, you want to fish tomorrow?"

"We'll see. Maybe in the evening. I gotta go down to the Sheriff's office sometime...and now the parade."

I looked Eddie right in the eyes. "Are you going to be alright?"

"Yeah. See you tomorrow."

I headed for the door with my head down. I didn't want to get involved in any more conversations. I stepped out on Loudoun St., took a deep breath, and returned my jacket collar to the upright position. My house was twelve blocks away and about a twenty-minute walk. It was a little quicker if I cut through the campus. With each passing block, the town got quieter, darker and a little colder. I put my hands in my jacket pockets and discovered the watch from the cabin. I had forgotten I took it with me. As I passed under a street light, I turned the band inside out and noticed an engraving – Frank Reynolds.

I walked along trying to figure out what happened to Liliana. Who killed her and why. Eddie? Why would he do it, and why at the river? It didn't make sense...Luis? Maybe.... Maybe he found out about her affair with Eddie. I was slowly convincing myself that neither one of them were guilty.

On the corner of Park and Stewart St., a small group of students were cooking up a late night snack on the grill.

'How could I get a burger?' I thought to myself. Ask them for directions? Say, "Have you seen my cat?, May I borrow a cup of sugar?"

I gave up on the idea and two blocks later I was home. The stars were incredible, and as I cut through my yard, I stepped on a can. Picking up a Natural Light can didn't surprise me at all. What did surprise me though, was that the can was icy cold, and that wasn't good.

8

Last night I slept like a baby. I was awake every hour or so tossing, turning, burping and farting. My last dream went something like this:

I met St. Peter at the golden gate. He was running my numbers and going over my past--good and bad. He showed me his list with my highlights and lowlights. It was very interesting to recall some of my past. In the eighth grade, I had found a wallet and returned it. I gave blood and donated to the Salvation Army regularly. However, I siphoned gas from old lady's cars in high school, had purposely driven through puddles to splash people after rain storms and my church attendance was sub par.

Anyway, Petey wasn't sure if I was accepted into Heaven or not. Some sort of grey area or he hadn't received all the information to make the proper decision. He was annoyed by the lack of info and taking it out on me. I wasn't exactly thrilled to be there even though he was the most famous person that I had yet to meet.

So we go to God's office to ask for clarification. The room is about twenty feet by twenty feet and lined with computers, maps and post it notes around the perimeter. God is sitting in an office chair with wheels rolling back and forth between computers. His hair is long and white, he's smoking and looks stressed out to the max. He is dealing with wildfires in the western U. S., cyclones in the far east, drought in Africa and starvation in Haiti. It reminded me of an air traffic controller up in the tower.

God finally notices us, stops what he's doing and says "Well?"

St. Peter says, "I got Steve Larkin here. He's on the fence. Could go either way. What do you think?"

"He gives wild flowers to young ladies for Christ's sake. Let him in."

The phone rang. It was Eddie. "You'll never guess what happened?"

"You're right. I'm not guessing."

"When I drove by the garage last night, on my way home, several lights were on. So, I parked on the side of the building and went in through the back door. Nobody there."

"Was there forced entry?"

"No. So, I cut the lights and started to call Skull when a cop car pulls up across the street. They killed the lights and just sat there staking out the place."

"Then what?"

"Well, I was tempted to sneak up on the cops and scare the shit out of them, but I was too tired. Skull didn't pick up so I figured why go home."

You slept at the shop?"

"Yeah. Well, I didn't sleep much. Must have taken a hundred three-minute naps. Anyway, get this."

"What?"

"I get up this morning, walk out to the Suburban and it has two flat tires. Both on the driver's side, slashed."

"No shit. Is my gear okay?"

"Yeah."

"What about Rocket?"

"He must have slept through it all."

"That's pretty strange," I said. "Somebody breaks in before you get there and leaves the lights on. And then someone comes by after you're there and slashes your tires. Lights are a pretty easy thing to remember to turn off."

"Exactly." Eddie came back with. "Maybe they were purposely left on."

"Do you need a ride?"

"Yeah, I do. I could use a ride home to get another vehicle. But first, I gotta go by the Sheriff's office. I called down there and they said they had some news for me. I still don't know where Skull is or I'd have her pick me up. Maybe she said she was going to her mother's house for the weekend. Hell I don't know."

I showered, left the house at 9:30 and welcomed another crisp, sunny morning. The frost from last night had burned off. Now I had another driving dilemma. Several streets were closed or modified for this morning's 10K race, a bicycle race, and the Sportsman's breakfast. And later this afternoon was the Grand Feature Parade. I finally arrived at the shop and Eddie and Rocket were in the parking lot sitting on top of a Corvair.

"How's it going?" I asked.

"I've felt better."

"Me too."

As my good friend R. Satterfield would say: "I have a headache that would kill a mule."

Eddie ran Rocket back in the shop, locked the door and got in my Bronco. I had a Joe Jackson CD waiting for him. I turned the wrong way out of the lot.

"Where are you going?" Eddie wanted to know.

"I need a big-ass Pepsi." I emphasized need.

"I hear you. I'm pretty thirsty," he said.

We entered Rileys convenience store and I drank half my Pepsi before I got to the counter. Before I could pay, a story in the upper right corner of the newspaper caught my eye.

A young woman, approximately 28 years of age, was found dead Friday evening near Back Creek off of Nelson's Ridge Road. She was carrying no identification. Anyone with information is encouraged to call the Frederick County Sheriff's Dept.

The Sheriff's Department was housed in the courthouse which took up an entire city block. However, due to an increase in misbehavior from the locals, outsiders, and students, they had outgrown their space. Winchester's exploding growth had earned it the reputation of being a bedroom community for Washington, DC. Since Winchester was close enough to DC for people to commute to work, it was also close enough for the DC criminals to commute the other way. The university had increased enrollment dramatically in the last several years to the point where I thought they were letting anyone in. The new Sheriff's department and jail was under construction across the street and scheduled to open by the end of the year.

Eddie and I entered the Sheriff's office on Cameron St. We made our way past the counter where several people were trying to bail out a friend or loved one for fighting or being drunk in public. If someone got bailed out early enough today they might still have enough time to get drunk before the Grand Feature Parade at 1:30 pm. We passed a room where a guy in a clown suit was being interrogated.

We finally arrived at Deputy Myers's office. Of all the deputies on the force, Eddie was most familiar with Greg Myers. They had played baseball together at

James Wood High School, and raced their cars against each other until Greg became a deputy.

"Eddie. I'm glad you're here. Sit down."

"Hey, Greg. You been busy?"

"Hell, yeah, we're busy. We've picked up our share of drunks and pickpockets. I got two whores from West Virginia locked up down stairs. Nobody is horny enough to bail them out. Let's see, there's been some personal property destroyed. And, it's only Saturday morning."

"Greg, this is Steve Larkin. He was with me yesterday.... He's actually my ride right now. I had some personal property destroyed last night too. You didn't arrest any tire-slashers, did you?"

"Nah. Stay put. A couple people want to talk to you. I'll be back."

After a few minutes, Deputy Myers returned with two gentlemen, one in uniform and one in street clothes. They sat on the edge of the table.

"Eddie, this is Sheriff Bob Wilkins and Malcolm Raines, the coroner."

The sheriff started off speaking ever so slowly. "Eddie Robinson. You're Art's boy aren't you?"

"That's right," Eddie said quickly.

"You had a rough day, yesterday. Found a body and had a gun pointed at you."

"Yes sir."

"Do you know the girl we hauled out of your place last night? A miss Liliana Tavarez."

"I know her. Knew her."

"How well did you know her?"

"Look, I told your deputies last night. She cleans for me at the garage every couple weeks. Her boyfriend, Luis, works for my old man at the orchard. He also works in my shop sometimes. So I see her around."

"Well, Malcolm here went over the body. You know she had a head wound."

"Yep. I noticed it."

"Nobody got into her pants which is good to know."

Eddie interrupted. "Sheriff, do you have any leads on who killed her?"

"Funny you said that."

"Said what?" Eddie was confused.

The sheriff stood up. "We're not positive she was killed."

"What the hell? You're not saying she's alive?"

"No. She's dead." The sheriff looked at the coroner. "Explain it to him Malcolm."

"Mr. Robinson, the cause of death was poisoning. She died of consuming too much methyl alcohol."

"Too much what?" Eddie wanted to know.

"Methanol. Wood alcohol. It usually happens when someone gets a hold of some bad moonshine."

"What about the head injury?" Eddie asked.

"Just for show. She may have stumbled around and fallen, but most likely someone struck her in the head after she was dead."

"What about the time of death?" I asked.

"Thursday. Sometime between 5:00 and 9:00 pm."

The sheriff butted in. "Eddie, do you keep any moonshine at that house, the house up there where the body was found?"

Eddie turned and looked at me, then looked straight down at the floor. He looked about as comfortable as a double agent sleeping on a Greyhound bus. Now I've had my share of Eddie's moonshine over the years. Not only does he keep some at the cabin, but I've seen it in the shop, at his house, and in his beer cooler. Once on a fishing trip in West Virginia, he traded a pint for a bag of ramps to a perfect stranger.

I don't drink much of it myself, but I do enjoy sampling the different flavors. My favorites are peach, plum and strawberry. Supposedly, Eddie always has the best. His connection is a guy who brings it up from Franklin County, the moonshine capital of Virginia.

Eddie turned toward the Sheriff. "Yes sir. I reckon I have a little bit at the cabin. "

"What do you say we take a ride out there and have a look around? Do some investigating."

"Fine by me," Eddie said. "Steve and I can meet you out there. Only thing, though, I have to be back to escort the mayor in the parade."

"Okay. Shouldn't take too long. Follow us and you'll get through town quicker."

"Oh, by the way, Sheriff. Greg said you were dealing with some destruction of property from yesterday. Well, if some of your re-election signs were run over, that might have been me. Nothing personal."

"Also, can you let Luis Ramirez go? I don't want to press any charges."

"I suppose so. He didn't hurt anybody."

I drove around the block and pulled into the lot where several squad cars were parked. We weren't sure which vehicle we were supposed to follow.

"Do you think she got into your moonshine? Maybe you got a bad batch." I asked.

"I don't know, man. I've never had a problem before."

Deputy Myers appeared, carrying what looked like two official police kits. Sheriff Wilkins was carrying a 16 oz. Styrofoam cup of coffee. They got in an unmarked 4-wheel- drive Jeep and led the way. We turned right on Cork Street, left on Braddock, and merged onto Valley Avenue. Whenever we came up on some street that was closed, some security person would move a sawhorse to let us through. The last sawhorse to be moved allowed us to cross over the bike race route on Jubal Early Drive, named for the famous Civil War general who thought about attacking Washington, DC, but changed his mind and took control of York, Pennsylvania. While there, the general presented city officials with a list of goods to be supplied to his troops, which included three days' rations, 2,000 pairs of shoes, 1,000 felt hats, 1,000 pairs of socks, and $100,000 in cash. Before long, we arrived at Eddie's cabin where Deputy Myers parked about 30 yards in front of it. I pulled in behind him.

We all jumped out and stood around looking at each other. Then Sheriff Wilkins started walking toward the cabin, keeping his eyes on the driveway.

The Sheriff asked, "What vehicles have been up here recently?"

Eddie said, "My Suburban and the Rescue Squad from last night. That's all I know of."

"Looky here, Myers. There are three different sets of tire tracks. Where did the Rescue Squad park?"

"Over there, sir." Eddie replied.

"Well, then, that explains this track."

They walked closer toward the cabin.

"Where did you park, Eddie?"

"Well, sir, I've been up here a couple times. I was here yesterday, of course, and I was here Thursday. I just park it wherever. Yesterday, we were in a pretty big hurry to get out of here. I reckon I slung a good bit of mud around."

The Sheriff continued to walk around with his head down. "It rained pretty hard Wednesday night, right?"

Eddie nodded.

"So these tracks should be from Thursday on."

"Should be," Deputy Myers interjected, trying to contribute to the investigation.

"Myers, looky here. This track here is repeated over and over. It's over there and over there and is fairly wide so it probably belongs to the Suburban. Now this third set of tracks looks to me like the vehicle was just here once. One set in and one set out. It's a narrower tire with street tread."

"I think you're right on Sheriff," Greg agreed.

"Go get the camera and the impression kit and we'll make some castings. Oh yeah, and bring some gloves and a box."

"You need some water?" I said.

"Yeah. I need a bucket of water, but I don't want you boys to go in the cabin just yet."

Deputy Myers returned and the sheriff instructed him on which tire tracks to photograph and make casts of. Then the four of us walked up to the cabin and entered.

"I'll take that water now. You got a bucket?"

Eddie quickly found a bucket in the kitchen and filled it. Deputy Myers was asked to go outside and make the plaster of Paris casts in the driveway.

"Alright now, Mr. Robinson, where's this moonshine that you might have here?"

"I've got a couple jars up there." Eddie said pointing at a cabinet.

"Show me, but don't touch them. I want to get the prints off the jars."

Eddie took a little step ladder out of a closet and opened the highest cabinet above the refrigerator.

"Oh shit!" Eddie blurted out.

"What?" I asked.

"There's three jars here."

"What?" I asked again.

"There's an extra jar."

"Don't touch them." The sheriff demanded.

Eddie leaned to his left so we could see. He pointed at the three jars.

"These two pint jars are mine. This jar here, I've never seen before."

Eddie's jars were mostly full while the one he claimed wasn't his, was nearly empty.

"I must say, Robinson, when you said you had some shine, I figured you had a case or two. I'm slightly disappointed."

Sheriff Wilkins put on a pair of latex gloves and placed the moonshine jars in a cardboard box.

"You might as well check out the dining room and take a look at this note." Eddie said.

He handed the note to the sheriff who didn't appear to be impressed.

"Anybody could have written that," he said. We'll take these jars back to town and run some tests. But first, show me around the rest of the house."

We walked through the house and stuck our heads in each room. Everything appeared to be in order except for the obvious damage to the dining room. We walked back through the kitchen and out onto the porch. Deputy Myers was finishing up the third cast.

"Steve, pull that door shut." Eddie said to me.

"Alright," the Sheriff said. "You guys can go. Oh, where is this Suburban? I want to match up your tire tread with the plaster casts."

"It's at my shop," Eddie said. Somebody stuck a knife in two of the tires. It's leaning to the left. You'll recognize it. It still has two good tires that you can match up unless somebody came by later this morning and slashed them, too."

The sheriff chuckled. "You *did* have a rough day yesterday."

9

"That third jar really wasn't yours?" I asked Eddie.

"Nope. Somebody planted it there. I'll bet you ten bucks to a doughnut that jar has methanol in it. Some bastard is trying to set me up. Frame me."

The Bronco rolled slowly down the driveway. We were both in deep thought trying to put the pieces together. We passed the cinder block shop, the pole barn and the spray shed. We were almost to the bridge when Eddie noticed a vehicle parked up the hill in the old Stayman block.

"Hey, drive up there." Eddie insisted.

"Who is it?"

"It's my old man. He's checking for damage from last night."

I parked behind Art's beat up Chevy Silverado pick-up truck. The tailgate was missing and it was obvious the truck had brushed against trees in the orchard for many years.

The apple flowers on these old trees were in the full bloom stage and quite beautiful. Also in bloom were the dandelions on the orchard floor. Dandelions and other weed flowers compete with the apple flowers for visits from honeybees. Before an apple can appear on a tree, the flower must first develop and open, be pollinated and ultimately fertilized. Honey bees are the major pollinator for fruit trees.

Being a horticulturist, I'm well aware of the havoc that freezing temperatures cause for growers. Full bloom is the stage when the flowers are most vulnerable to cold temperature injury. Though frost occurs at 32 degrees F, apple flowers become susceptible to damage at 28 degrees F. The duration of the cold period determines whether the flowers are damaged or killed.

The last frost date for the Shenandoah Valley is around May 10th which means there is a chance of frost until that date, every year. On a frost night, cold air runs downhill and settles in the lowest areas called frost pockets. Because of that, growers should plant orchards on their highest ground. There are some frost protection options, such as wind machines, but they aren't common around here. Most local growers turn to prayer during the frost season. Pioneer Orchards has a mix of both good and poor sites.

We caught up with Art. He was wearing a long sleeved shirt and a wide brimmed straw hat. He had a big chew of Mail Pouch tobacco in his left cheek and was unshaven. His Dalmatian was chasing insects. Art was pinching flowers to see if the ovaries were still alive. If it was still green it was alive. If a brown spot developed in the middle of the ovary, it was dead.

The ovary, along with the stigma and style, make up the female part of the flower. The ovary is surrounded by the male parts of the flower, anthers and filaments. The male parts are no help to a freezing ovary. They offer no hugging or cuddling and thus no warmth to the vulnerable ovary.

When an ovary freezes, all hell breaks loose. The cell walls breakdown which leads to ruptured membranes. Ultimately, the organelles in the cytoplasm spill out. It's a harsh and gruesome death.

"How's it lookin pop?"

"Not too bad out here. There's more damage closer to town."

"How cold did it get?"

"It was 26 at the house," Art said right away. "How you doing, Steve?"

"Good. You normally have a little damage each year. Don't you?"

"This is more than a little damage. And, it's coming again tonight." Art said.

"That's not good." I said.

Eddie interrupted. "Did you read the paper this morning?"

"Not yet."

"Let me give you the heads up."

"You mean about Liliana?"

"Oh, so you know."

"Yep. Some deputy phoned me last night. Woke me up. So what really happened?"

"I don't know, Dad. Steve and I got up with Sheriff Wilkins. We're trying to figure it out. Look, I need to get back to town. I've been asked to give the mayor a ride today in the parade and I don't even know if the Chevelle will start."

"Okay. Keep me posted. Oh, Linda phoned last night, too. Said she heard you might be in some trouble."

"Did she say where she was?"

"No. She didn't say."

We got back in the Bronco. Eddie wanted to continue up the hill instead of turning around. At the top was a terrific view of the Blue Ridge Mountains to the east. Today, due to a lack of haze, the view was spectacular.

"Always wanted to build a house up here." Eddie admitted.

"Nice spot."

"See that clearing over there?"

"Yeah. Put the house there?"

"Nah. That's where I set out a few pot plants every year."

"Really? Aren't you afraid of getting busted?"

"Hell no! The amigos are up here all the time. They'll get blamed before I will."

"Which way?" I asked.

"Keep going. This way comes out on the main road eventually."

The dirt road descended off the hill at a slight grade. We were surrounded by rows of apple trees for what seemed like a half mile. Eventually the road flattened out and intersected with a highway.

"Which way? I asked again.

"We should go right, but go straight instead. I want to check something out."

We crossed the highway and got back on another dirt road that was level for a couple hundred yards. As soon as the road started to go up, we found ourselves in another orchard. The trees were smaller and planted much closer together.

"I didn't know you guys had any blocks with dwarf trees. This is pretty impressive."

"We don't. We left Pioneer Orchards on the other side of the highway. This is Pete Bannister's orchard. He's one of the more progressive growers in the area. He's growing modern varieties on dwarfing rootstocks. I hear he's doing well. That's because he's still young and energetic."

We topped the hill and admired the view. About fifty yards ahead was a van parked on the right side of the road between two rows of trees.

"Who's that?" I asked.

"Amigos, I reckon! Looks like they're pruning. Lily's brother, Juan, works for Pete. The pruning season should be over. They must be behind."

"They work Saturdays?" I asked, knowing the answer.

"Ole Buddy, they'd work every day if you'd let them. They hate to take a day off. They send most of their money to family back in Mexico, so they work as much as they can."

"Steve, slow down. Pass the van and then stop on the other side. I want all of them to get a good look at me."

I passed the baby blue Ford van. In the back window was a bumper sticker that read: Support Your State Police. Eddie lowered the window as I came to a stop. Six small Mexicans were pruning. They were piling the brush in the drive middles to be bush-hogged later. Eddie stuck his head out of the window and yelled.

"Que pasa! Trabajar duro." He looked at me. "Shit. I think I just told them to work harder. I meant to say are you working hard." He leaned out the window and yelled again. "Tu eres muy trabajador?"

We could hear some grumbling. "Duro bastante." One of them yelled.

"Que' ha ocurrido Liliana?" Another yelled. They were getting riled up.

"Fue usted?"

"Fue Luis?"

Two of them started walking toward us.

"Fue usted?" One yelled again.

"Vete al Diablo!"

"Go." Eddie said. "Drive slowly, though. I don't want them to think we're scared."

I pulled away. "What did they say?" I wanted to know.

"They said, What happened to Liliana? Was it you? Was it Luis? I think one said get the hell out of here."

"Was Juan there?"

"I didn't recognize him."

I drove along slowly for about thirty seconds. Then Eddie said, "That accomplished a couple things. First, they know about Lily which means every Hispanic in the county probably knows. Second, they don't know who killed her either. And, since they mentioned Luis, they haven't ruled out the killer might be Mexican.

10

I fumbled with my compact disk case as I drove off the hill and inserted J. J. Cale's "Troubadour" disk and turned right on some county road which ended abruptly at Route 522. We turned right, towards town. As we approached the Route 37 bypass, I realized that we were on the bike race route when we passed a tight group of cyclists. Eddie grabbed the steering wheel and blew the horn several times. Some poor son-of-a-bitch shot off the road and down into the weeds he went. Eddie laughed.

"What the hell?" I yelled. Eddie couldn't stop laughing.

"Steve, do you know why those biker dudes wear tight black shorts?"

"You tell me."

"So when they get the shit scared out of them, no one can tell."

Eddie laughed again. I looked in the rearview mirror and several cyclists had their arms raised with fists clinched, cussing me out. Right when I thought they might come after me, they veered onto the bypass and headed south. They had about three miles to go before the race ended at Handley High School.

"You idiot." I yelled at Eddie. "What if they got my plate number?"

"Ah settle down. They didn't see your plate. And, besides, there must be twenty black Broncos in town."

I slowed down as Route 522 turned into Fairmont Ave. I was relieved to see that no cyclists were tailing me. I pulled into Eddie's parking lot and we both glanced over at the Suburban. It was still leaning to the left. I parked in front of the first garage door.

"Are you going to put tires on your vehicle?

"Nah. Not now. I don't have any here that are the right size. The tire stores are probably closed and besides, I gotta get the Chevelle running and cleaned up."

"Oh, yeah. Well, if you want some help later, let me know."

"Let's go in the front door this time and see what surprises we find." Eddie said.

"Okay, but unlock the Suburban. I want to grab my stuff out of it."

Eddie watched me as I gathered up my gear and shoved it in the Bronco. Nothing was missing. We walked around to the front of the shop. Taped to the front door was a large white envelope from Mercer Realty. Eddie removed the envelope and unlocked the door. The bell rang as we entered. Rocket made a move toward us but immediately retreated when he realized who it was. Eddie flipped on some lights and opened the envelope.

"What the hell is this?" he said.

"What is it?

"It's a letter and a business card and some other crap from Mercer Realty. Get a load of this."

Eddie began to read:

Attention Edward Robinson,

This letter is in response to your request for information regarding the sale and development of Pioneer Orchards. It is my understanding that your desire is to sell off and develop portions of the property in increments as opposed to selling the entire property outright. I have taken the maps that you provided and divided your orchard blocks into three-, five-, and ten-acre tracts. I feel these various sized tracts are the most desirable sized parcels for future homeowners in that part of Frederick County.

It is my opinion that your sixty-acre Marshall block, located between Apple Pie Ridge and Spruce Run Road, would be the logical first property to develop due to its proximity to existing infrastructure and the city of Winchester.

At your convenience, please schedule an appointment at my office to discuss this matter further. I feel this will be an exciting venture for you and will benefit future home owners in Frederick County. Thank you for choosing Mercer Realty for the opportunity to work with you in this endeavor.

Sincerely,

Brian Mercer

"Now don't that beat all! Who does that bastard think he is?"

"What's that all about?" I asked.

"That Brian Mercer.... He's a God Damn renegade. He's runs around the county trying to convince farmers to develop their land."

"Let me guess. You didn't request that information."

"Bingo!.....I'm starting to think I'm on Candid Camera."

Eddie shook his head and started walking toward the office. He picked up the phone and checked his messages while I gazed at pictures of topless girls bent over sports cars.

Eddie put the phone down and said, "I gotta make a couple calls," as he motioned me away. "I'll meet you over by the Chevelle."

"Okay. I need to take a leak."

I turned the corner and walked toward the disgustingly dirty unisex restroom. I opened the door but closed it without entering. I leaned toward the office and could barely hear Eddie talking to someone.

"I know. I know. I said I would have it yesterday.... I need a little more time.... Early next week. I promise.... You tell him the same thing."

Eddie apparently hung up and made another call.

" Hey man. It's me. I'm feelin the heat here.... A couple guys are breathing down my neck.... ASAP.... Later."

WhenI heard the phone hit the counter. I opened the restroom door and pretended to walk out. Eddie passed me and I followed him toward the fourth bay. We had to step over and walk around stacks of wheels, boxes of parts, and fifty-five gallon drums of oil. He took a deep breath, and then gently began pulling the cover off of his most prized possession. I sensed that he thought perhaps whoever was in the shop yesterday might have messed with the car. He let out a sigh of relief.

Eddie pushed the automatic garage door opener on the wall. As the door slowly rose, the sunlight revealed the glossy black paint. The top was down. Eddie got in and quickly found the ignition key on his oversized key ring. He turned the key and much to his surprise, it fired right up. He revved the engine over and over again, pulled it outside and shut her down. He climbed out and put a dip of snuff behind his lower lip. I had seen that big smile before whenever he would hit a big out in darts or catch a nice trout.

"Alright! It started. That'll save me some time. Now all I got to do is hose it off."

"It sure is a pretty car. You've obviously taken great care of it." I remarked.

"Yep. It's my baby. Look at those leather seats. Used to get a lot of ass in that backseat. No one has driven it but me in the last fifteen years or so."

"Wow! Really? Can I drive it?" I said, seriously.

"Don't you mean, May I drive it?"

"Good one." I said.

Eddie held up his key ring. "There's only one key. You'll have to fight me for it. Hey! Why don't you ride along."

"In the parade? With you and the mayor?"

"Sure. You can ride shotgun. The mayor can sit on top of the back seat so he can wave to everybody. It'll be fun."

"What the hell. I don't have anything else to do. I've never ridden in a parade before. Maybe we'll meet Willard Scott."

The phone began to ring and Eddie walked off toward the office. I grabbed the hose and carefully rinsed off the car even though it really didn't need it. I picked up the cleanest rag in the shop I could find and dried it off.

"That was the sheriff," Eddie said when he came back. "He said that extra jar of moonshine had enough wood alcohol in it to kill a horse."

"That's what you figured."

"The car looks great. Thanks." Eddie said, smiling.

The clock on the wall was so dusty that you could barely make out that both hands were pointed toward the twelve.

"Is that clock right?" I asked.

"Pretty close."

"Are you going home and get cleaned up or what?"

"Nah. I'll just take a Polish shower here. I got a couple clean shirts in the back. Besides, I'm starving. Let's get something to eat."

"When does the parade start?"

"One-thirty, but I need to be down there by one o'clock."

"Where?" I asked.

"Where? How long have you lived in this town? The Grand Feature Parade starts at the corner of Cork and Cameron Streets."

"Sorry. I'm no parade expert."

"No shit!"

Eddie walked off toward the office and was gone for several minutes. He returned wearing a long sleeve, black western shirt with pearl snaps. The lapels were embroidered with a Royal Flush - Spades. He wore a stiff, white western hat with a black band and was carrying a small cooler.

"What are you *doing*?" I asked him. "You went from Dr. Jekyll to Mr. Rodeo."

"You gotta look the part."

"All I have is this green L. L. Bean chamois shirt," I said.

"Steve, you look great. Come on, we need to hurry if we're going to eat."

"What's in the cooler?"

"I grabbed a few beers. These parades can go on forever."

"Moonshine?" I asked sarcastically.

"No moonshine."

"Where to?" I asked.

"What are you thinkin'?"

"You're driving." I reminded him.

"Get in. I'll surprise you."

Eddie slapped the garage door button and we ran outside before the door hit us in the head. He locked the front door, put the cooler in the backseat and we were off. The radio belted out a Beach Boys song.

"What's this?" I asked.

"Oldies. I play oldies whenever I drive the Chevelle."

Bright sunshine was bearing down on us. We pulled out onto Fairmont Avenue and were immediately stopped in heavy traffic. Straight ahead of us was a float carrying the Winchester/Frederick County Beauty Pageant Winners. The float was covered with thousands of apple blossoms made from pink and white crepe paper. The girls were seated and wore long green expensive dresses. They cradled bouquets of pink roses. None of them were practicing their waving.

Eddie blew the horn and waved to the girls. He took some side streets over to Berryville Avenue and headed west. We circled around Mount Hebron Cemetery and turned south on Pleasant Valley Road.

Eddie took a right on Stanwick Street and pulled into a small dirt parking lot behind a little white cinder block building. He drove slowly not to kick up the dust and parked next to a chain link fence covered in honeysuckle. Also parked in the lot was an early 80s, copper colored, Pontiac Grand Prix with a severely weathered rag top. Parked next to it was a late 70s Ford Van with a "Support Your State Troopers" bumper sticker in the rear window.

"Where the hell are we?" I wanted to know.

"You don't know do you?" Eddie asked. "We're behind Casitas."

"Where?" I was confused.

"Casitas Mexican Food Store." Eddie said proudly.

"Are you crazy?" I asked but knew the answer. "Mexican Food Store? Are you going to stir up some trouble?"

"Hell no... I want to eat. They make homemade pork tamales on Saturdays. Come on."

I jumped out and gently closed the door. I asked "Will your car be okay parked out here?"

"Sure. We won't be in there long. Hey grab two beers out of the cooler. They don't sell beer here."

As I bent over the car to retrieve the beers, I noticed the tire tracks in the soft moist dirt behind the car. I had seen those tracks before. Unfortunately, I had seen them just this morning. At the cabin.

11

I was confused. I felt I had just discovered a clue that could incriminate Eddie for the death of Liliana, which I should report, and yet Eddie was willing to walk into a, perhaps hostile, Mexican store and search for clues as if he is innocent. I decided to keep it under my belt and conduct some detective work myself. As my good friend R. Satterfield would say: "It was time to dummy up."

Outside Casitas front door two dogs were hoping someone would toss them a snack. We entered the store and every head turned toward us. My head rose several inches above the top of the shelves so I could follow everyone's move. Eddie walked ever so slowly toward the counter while I took a different route. All eyes were on Eddie. I was nervous and felt out of place. However, the store smelled really good. From fresh the tamales, I was assuming.

The store was stocked with canned vegetables, hot sauces, spices, tortillas and dry beans and other Hispanic delights. Most of the labels were in Spanish. On the counter you could find magazines and cigars. Behind the counter were the adult movies, translated into Spanish. Two young boys were enjoying a Mexican can of soda and smiling like it was Christmas. Eddie was his usual cool self.

"Que pasa?" Eddie yelled to anyone who'd listen.

No one said a word as Eddie walked up to the counter. The proprietor, Carlos, had a three-inch scar on his left cheek and looked like he'd led a pretty rough life. He gave us a nod.

"Buenas tardes." Eddie blurted out with confidence.

"Buenas tardes, Senor Robinson. Are you hungry?"

"Yeah. My buddy and I want some tamales."

"How many?"

Eddie glanced at me and then back at him. "Seis!"

"What sauce?"

"Caliente, por favor."

"You eat them here?"

"Sure. Hey, this is Steve. He teaches at the college. Well, we're not really sure what he does at the college."

Carlos went back into the kitchen and the other patrons went back to doing what they came in the store for in the first place. Eddie popped open our two cans of Busch Light. Carlos returned with six steaming tamales wrapped in corn husks. He squirted some red sauce on a small plate. I unwrapped one, dipped it in the sauce and took a big bite. Every Mexican restaurant in America claims to serve authentic food but this stuff was for real.

"These are awesome!" I said with my mouth full.

"I told you."

"How come you never brought me here before?"

"Cause we fish together. We're not in a lunch club."

Carlos butted in. "Any news on what happened to Liliana?"

Eddie's head jerked around. "No. We're workin' on it, though."

"Luis was in here earlier. He has...how do you say...temper? He say you get him out of jail."

"What did he want?" Eddie was curious to know.

"I don't know. He made a couple phone calls, slammed a couple beers and left. He was walkin'."

Eddie took a bite and then scratched his head. "It's a mess, Carlos. Luis thinks I killed Liliana, I thought Luis killed her, and the sheriff says it could have been an accident."

Occasionally Eddie took a look over his shoulder but there would be no trouble from the store patrons today. We polished off our tamales. Eddie picked up an empty used cup, stuffed a napkin in it and dropped a ten dollar bill on the counter.

"Thanks, Carlos. If I hear anything I'll let you know. You do the same?"

Carlos nodded in agreement.

We left the store very content but the dogs were disappointed to see us walk away.

"That went well--I think. Nobody stabbed me, or even yelled at me," Eddie said with confidence.

"Hey look over there." Eddie pointed.

"What?"

"Over there. There's more of those crotch keys that you like to give away."

"Oh, cool." I said.

In the corner of the lot along the fence, several two-feet tall Blue Flag Irises were in full bloom. I took out my pocket knife and removed five of them. Then I cut them back to about eighteen inches.

We got in the car and looked at each other. Eddie fired it up, revved it up and backed it out onto Stanwick Street. After two blocks we turned right on Cameron Street. As we eased toward Cork Street, both sides of the street were clogged with floats, bands and rescue vehicles trying to figure out where they were supposed to be. It looked like a real cluster fuck.

"Hey, where are we supposed to go?" I said.

"We're behind the Boy Scouts. Troop 42--my old troop. Just look for the Scouts."

"Will they be on Cameron or Cork?"

"I can't remember. The mayor told me to meet him behind the scout troop. Cameron I think. We're pretty close to the beginning, which is good cause it will be over sooner."

Eddie crept along weaving in and out of the chaos. We passed the American Legion Local, Bill's Wrecking tow truck, the Salvation Army Float, and the Knights of Columbus. The Winchester Karate Club was practicing their chops and kicks.

"Look. There's Gary," I yelled toward Eddie. "Hey Gary…. Come here. Come here a minute."

He walked over and leaned on my side of the car and shook his head.

"This looks like trouble," he blurted out.

"Watch it." Eddie said. "We are in trouble. Well, I am."

"I heard."

He glanced at the cooler and shook his head again. Eddie and I both knew Gary, the Frederick County Agent, pretty well. Gary had visited Pioneer Orchards numerous times over the last twenty years. He had coordinated several fruit grower meetings there on the farm.

I knew Gary more from the ornamental side of horticulture. He had his work cut out for him. Because besides working with the fruit and vegetable growers, he also works with the nursery and greenhouse producers in the county. And with the housing market booming, the landscaping industry was growing by leaps and bounds.

Also, Gary was an occasional guest speaker in my Landscape Management and Nursery Crops courses. He had a knack for explaining the opportunities that await students in the green industry. Hard work and long hours are in store. His concluding statement, was something like 'You got to love what you do because you probably won't get rich doing it.'

I put my hand on his shoulder.

"Gary, we're looking for the Boy Scouts. Have you seen them?"

"42?"

"Yeah."

He pointed toward Cork Street. "They're up there about a block."

"Thanks, man."

"Hey, Eddie, sorry to hear about what happened. Actually I don't know what happened."

"Neither do I," Eddie said. "Neither do I."

"Oh, by the way, how's Art?"

"You know Art. He won't show it, but between what happened yesterday and the frost last night, I figure he's pretty upset."

The driver of a flatbed truck, sponsored by Virginia Farm Credit, blew his horn behind us. I patted Gary on the shoulder.

"We better get moving. Thanks."

We continued weaving past floats and politicians. Eddie blew the horn and sent the James Wood High School Band running for the sidewalks. He laughed. We eased around the Marine Corps Mounted Color Guard and found ourselves directly behind a group of boys in green uniforms donning merit badge sashes.

"Made it," Eddie said with a sigh of relief, and shut the engine off.

"Did you smell those horses?" I asked.

"That was awful. Good thing we're ahead of them."

"You know how ironic this is, don't you?" I asked.

"What do you mean?" Eddie asked.

"Just think. Yesterday afternoon we left town to avoid all this shit and now we couldn't be any deeper in it."

"You're right. Hey, look. There's the mayor."

Ray Carpenter, the reigning mayor of Winchester, presides over town council which is made up of nine councilmen from four wards. Council meets twice a month to discuss and vote on typical city problems such as budgets, zoning and what to do with the vagrants and homeless. Ray was pretty well liked throughout the city and claimed to be a man of the people, all the people. Perhaps that is why he was drinking at the Crystal Bar last night. Today, however, he was sporting the typical festival garb and carrying a brief case.

"Eddie, where have you been? I thought I was going to have to hitchhike down the parade route."

"Relax ol' buddy. Hey, meet Steve Larkin. He teaches at the college. He's going to ride along with us. See a parade from the inside looking out."

Ray pulled two signs out of his briefcase which read 'Ray Carpenter, Mayor of Winchester, VA.

"Eddie, here's some tape, attach these to your vehicle." Eddie did what he was told.

"Are they straight?"

"Yeah they're straight. Jump in. Sit up there. Hell it's after 1:30. It's probably started."

The mayor sat up on his perch and said, "This is nice." He was excited.

Bands were warming up ahead of us. Some of the scouts were sitting in the street waiting for their turn to shine. Then we heard a horn from a fire truck over on Braddock Street. The parade was underway.

Eddie put in a dip of snuff, straightened his hat and fired it up. He looked over at me and blew the horn. Three scouts jumped to their feet. I shook my head.

"Okay Mayor, this is it. You ready?"

"Let's roll."

"Try not to fall off."

We eased up Cameron and turned left on Cork, the official start of the parade route. Then we just sat there for five minutes.

The first half of the parade meanders through Old Town passing by some city government buildings and many small businesses. Attorney's offices and a few apartments occupy row houses scattered around on the narrow streets. The lots and courtyards are small and quaint.

The second half of the parade passes through the oldest and wealthiest neighborhood in town. Wide Victorian style mansions, with towering gables, line both sides of Washington Street. These homes have decent sized front yards, making them ideal for hosting parade parties with a close up view of the action. Large wrap-around porches are a refuge for spectators wanting to retreat to higher ground for a better view or to escape the sun. It was very prestigious to attend and be seen at a parade party on Washington Street.

Spectators lining the first half of the parade route were more likely to drink Thunderbird wine and pick apples, while spectators on Washington Street were more likely to drink Pinot Grigio and own the apples.

We crossed Loudoun Street and turned right on Braddock where red, white and blue banners hung from second story balconies. Temporary bleachers were erected in areas where they would fit and the traffic lights were blinking yellow. The sidewalks were packed with young families with small coolers and balloons tied to their strollers. Kids and parents were reaching for all the candy and free crap that was thrown at them. Nobody was too excited to see us until Ray opened his briefcase.

"You guys want a tootsie roll or a double bubble before I run out?"

Eddie held up his spit cup. "Nah."

The mayor began tossing candy in both directions which quickly got everyone's attention. People were yelling "Over here".... "Hey mayor".... "I love you, man." He was eating it up. We slowly rolled by the Rexall Drug store on the corner of Wolfe Street, the shoe store on the corner of Boscowen Street, and turned left on Piccadilly. The flow was backed up and we ended up sitting right in front of O'Blivions.

"Are you thinking what I'm thinking?" I asked Eddie.

"Yep. You better get in there."

I grabbed the flowers on the floor, straightened them up, and ran into the bar.

"Where's he going?" The mayor asked Eddie.

"He'll be right back. He has a delivery to make. Hey, Mayor, where is the mayor of Winchester, England?"

"There's a new guy this year. He wanted to walk. I think he's behind us."

When I came out, Eddie was creeping along and I had to run to catch up with him.

"Was she in there?" Eddie asked.

"Nope. She works tonight. Travis said he would make sure she got them."

We turned left onto Washington Street and Eddie requested a beer from the mayor. We worked our way through the route. The mayor must have been running out of candy because the intervals between throws were increasing. As we rolled along, Eddie checked out the crowd and waved to an occasional acquaintance. He seemed to know as many people as the mayor. We crossed Cecil Street and came to a stop while some band was performing for the judges a couple blocks ahead of us. I could smell the horses.

"Well son-of-a-bitch," Eddie blurted out. "I see Brian Mercer over there. I'll be right back."

Eddie put the gear in neutral and depressed the emergency brake. He laid his hat on the seat and jumped out. He pushed his way through the crowd and walked right up to Brian and started letting him have it. I couldn't hear what he was saying, but he was yelling and had his finger pointed in his face. The mayor kept on waving to the crowd. He was calm and acted like he had experienced this before.

Then, two women sneaking away from the scene caught my eye. The taller one wore tight green shorts and a large pink hat. It was Skull. The two of them slipped through the crowd and disappeared.

The scouts began to move forward and I thought I was going to get my chance to drive the Chevelle. Just then Eddie returned. The crowd was booing him, so he turned around and gave them double fingers. He jumped in and caught up with the scouts. He was steaming.

"What did he have to say for himself?" I asked.

"The prick said he got a written request in the mail, along with topographic maps, to start designing a housing development on the orchard."

"Do you think he made it up?"

"Hell I don't know. I didn't send him anything. I don't know anything anymore."

We rolled along slowly. Eddie was deep in thought. I decided to keep quiet about the Skull sighting. We crossed Leicester Street and then came to a stop again.

"Hurry up and wait," I said, trying to resume a conversation.

"It's almost over now," Eddie said. "We gotta make a right up here and then a left on Stewart Street. Then we make a left on Handley Boulevard, pass the judges' stand and it ends at the high school."

We started rolling again. Out of nowhere someone pounded on the trunk and jumped up on the backseat behind Eddie. "What the hell," we all thought, and turned to check out who our new passenger was. It was Luis with two Mexican dudes flanking each side of the car.

"Uh-oh," I said. "Here we go again."

"Who are you?" The mayor asked as he scooted over. Luis ignored him.

"Eddie," Luis said, "I checked out your alibi."

Eddie engaged the clutch, hit the brake and the car came to an abrupt stop. The scouts kept walking. Luis leaned forward until he was right behind Eddie's head.

"I talk with your bowling buddies. They say you bowl but you come late. Maybe one hour late. Why you late Eddie?"

Eddie stuttered a little. "I had to run an errand...out of town. It took a while longer than I thought it was going to."

I tapped Eddie on the leg and pointed toward the big gap between us and the scouts.

"No errand," Luis yelled. "You were with Liliana, yes?"

Eddie turned slowly toward the backseat. "What do you think, Mayor?" Eddie extended his right arm to the mayor as if to shake hands. The mayor stuck out his arm and Eddie grabbed his wrist as tight as he could. He popped the clutch as he stomped on the accelerator, the car lunged forward, Luis rolled off the trunk and hit the pavement. Hard.

12

"That's it. We're outta here. You better sit on the seat, Mayor."

Eddie drove up behind the leery scouts. They were walking forward but looking back behind them. He motioned for them to move toward the sidewalks. They obliged and we passed right through them. We turned right onto German Street and passed a rescue truck from Stephens City on the right and someone in a Ronald McDonald costume on the left. Eddie was sporadically tooting the horn.

I looked behind us and saw no sign of Luis or his entourage. The Marine Corps Mounted Color Guard should have caught up with him by now.

"Mayor, do you want to jump out?" Eddie asked.

"Nah. Keep going. Just don't hit anybody."

We turned left on Stewart Street and Eddie sent the Berryville Middle School cheerleaders into a frenzy. They screamed and tossed their pom poms into the air. As we weaved through the Fruit of the Loom characters the Bunch of Grapes stumbled and had to roll toward the sidewalk.

By now the parade participants ahead of us were sensing the panic and were moving off to the side of the street before we arrived. Eddie slowed down and cruised down the middle of the street. The mayor climbed up on the top of the backseat and began waving again. Some people cheered but most didn't know what to make of it.

We turned left on Handley Boulevard, the last leg of the parade. Bands, floats, politicians, the Shriners and the Grand Marshal, Willard Scott, were all pulled off to one side of the street or the other. Ahead, in plain view, were the reserved seating bleachers, the judges' stand and a bunch of cops that aren't usually there. Everyone was standing up with their eyes on us.

"Check that out, Steve."

"What?" I said, nervously.

"Those bleachers. Can you believe people pay money to sit there and watch this crap."

"This may be my first parade, but they can't all be this exciting. I think they'll be talking about this one for a long time."

Eddie looked me in the eyes. "I reckon you're right."

Eddie spit in his cup and said "Hey, Mayor, you want to ride along with me again next year?"

"I'll think about it," the mayor said and chuckled.

"Okay. Let's get this over with."

We rolled passed the bleachers and Eddie stopped in front of the judges. They were dumbfounded.

"How'd we do?" Eddie yelled up at them. They just stared at us in disbelief.

Eddie looked at me and then back at the judges. He yelled again.

"We started out around thirtieth place and finished-- what? In the top ten? Not bad if you ask me."

The cops motioned for us to proceed, and by looking at their faces, I could tell they were more than ready for us to get the hell off the parade route. Sheriff Wilkins motioned Eddie off the street and made him pull onto the worn out grass on the high school property. Eddie parked, turned down the radio and removed his hat. We were swarmed by several deputies. I heard a band start up behind us and assumed the parade had commenced again. Sheriff Wilkins walked up and put both hands on the driver's side door.

"Eddie, we meet again. Steve, how you doin'? Mr. Mayor, how was your ride?"

"Not bad. Entertaining! I ran out of candy though."

"Alright. What happened Eddie?" The sheriff demanded.

"We were just rolling along, and then all of a sudden Luis jumps in the back of the car and we were surrounded by the amigos. Then he starts questioning me."

"Was he armed?" The sheriff asked.

"I don't know. He was last night, as you know." Eddie said.

The sheriff was checking out everyone's body language while listening to Eddie's explanation. "Go on."

"Next thing I know, Luis falls off the back of the car. He must have been drunk or something. I didn't recognize any of those other guys with him so I became concerned for the mayor's safety. I figured we can't have the mayor of Winchester attacked, especially today, the biggest day of the year for this town. So I decided I better get the mayor to safety and well, here he is. He's all yours, Sheriff. Safe and sound."

"He saved my life," the mayor blurted out.

"Ah, shucks, Mayor. I just postponed your death."

Sheriff Wilkins looked straight at me.

"Well?

"That's what happened," I said. "Eddie's a hero," I added.

The sheriff shook his head. "Hero my ass."

The deputies were losing interest by all the bullshit and walked off one by one. The mayor slid off the side of the car and landed on his feet. "May I go now, Bob?" he said to the sheriff.

"Sure, Ray. You can go. You need a ride?"

"No, thanks. I think I'll walk for awhile. My ass is asleep."

Eddie jumped out. "You want these signs?"

"You can toss them. Thanks for the ride, Eddie. Good to meet you Steve."

"Good to meet you, Mayor. Don't forget your briefcase," I said.

Eddie removed the sign from his door and walked around the car. The sheriff followed him. He removed the sign from my door.

"This your car?" The sheriff asked while walking around and scrutinizing it.

"Yep. Had it since high school."

"Very nice. Where do you park it?"

"In the garage." Eddie said, cautiously.

"I'd like to come by the garage sometime and have a look around?"

"Sure. Steve and I are headed up there now, unless I'm under arrest."

"You run along. I better wait until after the parade. How about four o'clock? No, now that I think about it, actually, tomorrow would be better. How about ten o'clock tomorrow morning?"

Eddie and I looked at each other.

"Sure. We can meet you at the shop tomorrow morning," Eddie said.

"We? I'm going too?" I wanted to know.

"Steve. What else do you have to do?"

I looked at Eddie. "I don't know, sleep, fish, screw."

Eddie looked at the sheriff. "We'll be there."

"Eddie." The sheriff said in a serious tone. "Stay out of trouble tonight."

Eddie got back in the car, carefully put his hat back on his head and checked himself out in the mirror. He turned up the radio. The chorus to "Stand By Me" by Ben E. King rang out and Eddie turned up the volume. We sang as he drove off slowly, parallel to Handley Boulevard, remaining on the patchy grass and dirt to avoid the scattering crowd:

And darling, darling, stand by me
Darling, darling, stand by me
Whenever you're in trouble
Won't you stand by me, oh, stand by me

People were milling around trying to figure out where they were supposed to go next. Young girls were removing their high heels and baling off their floats. Exhausted band members were practically dragging their instruments. The lines were growing at the portable toilets. I looked back toward Sheriff Wilkins. He was kneeling down staring at the dirt where the Chevelle had been parked. I knew what he was up to.

13

We rolled down to Valley Avenue. Eddie turned to me and said, "Where to?"

"I think I'm sunburned," I said.

Eddie ignored me. "I reckon I better put the car away before something happens to it," he said. "Let's go back to the shop. Is that okay with you?"

"Sure."

Eddie's Garage was about a mile and a half north of the high school. He flung his snuff from his lip into the street and turned south. Eddie looked at me and grinned.

"We better go around. It'll be a sombitch trying to get through town."

"You're driving." I said.

Eddie pulled out in front of a tractor pulling a float carrying the disc jockeys from WINC. We drove about a mile down Valley Avenue to the intersection of Weems Lane where Eddie pulled into Clark's convenient store.

"I need to make a couple calls. But first, I gotta piss like a race horse."

I became excited. "Race horse!" I shouted. "The Derby is in a couple hours."

"I know. And I haven't put any bets down yet. I gotta do that. You need anything?" Eddie asked.

"I'll go with you. I need to stretch my legs."

We made our way toward the store. Two young girls flew out the door with Slurpees. Eddie hobbled in ahead of me and made a bee line for the restroom. I had never been inside before so I cruised up and down the aisles looking for unusual items. I found sardines, pork rinds and moon pies. The live bait was kept in the same cooler as the bologna and Velveeta cheese. The sign above the hot dog roller read "Buy 3 For The Price Of 3." Near the counter I discovered adult magazines, caffeine pills, headache powder, and lucky rabbit's feet.

The young girl behind the counter was flipping through a *National Enquirer* while twirling her hair. She appeared bored and irritated that she had to work today. She finally looked up and acknowledged me.

"You need any help?"

"No. I'm just waiting on my buddy. Pretty quiet around here?"

"Yep. We were busy earlier. Everybody must be at the parade. Speaking of the parade, the guy on the radio, broadcasting the parade, just said some maniac in a black Chevrolet sports car was driving around passing bands and floats and scaring the hell out of everybody."

"Really?" I said, just as Eddie showed up beside me.

"Did you hear that?" I asked Eddie.

"No.... What?"

"She said the guy broadcasting the parade on the radio said there was some maniac in a sports car terrorizing everyone in the parade."

"You don't say. What kind of sports car?" Eddie asked.

"Black Chevy."

"You don't say. There are some nuts out there."

We turned toward the door just as a middle-aged scruffy looking dude, wearing dirty camouflage clothes, carrying a backpack and walking stick, entered the store. Eddie and I watched the guy enter the Men's room.

Eddie shook his head. "Poor bastard."

"What? Do you think that guy is homeless?" I said.

"Shit, I don't know. I'm talking about the restroom. I blew it up."

We walked outside and I raised my head to intercept the sun's warm rays, forgetting that I was already sunburned. Eddie entered the phone booth, dropped in a quarter and punched in a number. I milled around the car hoping to listen in on his conversation. I opened the cooler and removed two beers. I looked at Eddie just as he hung up the receiver. He retrieved the quarter, dropped it in again and punched in another number. I held up a beer and he motioned for me to bring it to him. As I opened the door, I saw Eddie's face light up.

"Really? He's there now? Awesome! I can be there in fifteen minutes."

He slammed down the phone and grabbed the beer from me.

"Let's roll."

"What's going on?"

"Skull wasn't home, as usual. But the good news is that my racing fuel showed up. The truck is at the garage."

We pulled back out on Valley Avenue, headed south, turned east on Nichols Creek Grade and merged onto the Route 37 bypass headed north. Eddie took his hat off and punched the throttle. We reached 80 MPH in no time. We blew by an Airstream trailer. The family was probably burned out from the weekend and headed home a little early. We passed two floats fleeing the city. Both were spewing crepe paper all over the highway.

Eddie shot across two lanes and exited the bypass at the Route 522 intersection. The same intersection where he caused a cyclist to veer off the road and who most likely shit his drawers. We turned right and headed toward the shop as we had done just a few hours before.

Eddie cruised past the garage and turned in the lot on the far side where his Suburban was parked. He drove around back and there, parked next to the shed, protruding from the shop, was an International flatbed truck with what looked like a 500-gallon tank on the bed. Eddie waved to the driver, drove around to the front of the shop and backed the Chevelle up to the fourth bay garage door. He shut her down, jumped out, tossed his hat on the seat and scurried toward the truck. I had trouble keeping up with him.

"Donnie!" Eddie yelled. "Am I glad to see you."

"Eddie. How you doing? Nice shirt."

"Better now. I can't believe you drove up here this weekend. I figured I wouldn't see you til Monday at the earliest."

"We knew you were out. It's been crazy lately. We can't keep up with demand."

"Well, you're here now. How much you got?"

"Should be about 200 gallons in there. I had a stop in Harrisonburg earlier. I tried to save you 200 gallons."

Eddie unlocked the pad lock on the shed door and went inside closing the door behind him. Donnie was 6' 5" tall and must have weighed 400 lbs. He was dressed like a lumberjack. He sported a long red beard and his large belly stretched his bib overalls. As my good friend R. Satterfield would say: "He looked like he didn't have enough sense to piss in the tall weeds."

He placed the hose from his truck through the porthole on the shed. About twenty seconds later, Eddie yelled from inside "Let her go." Donnie started the pump, turned a ball valve ninety degrees and yelled back "On the way." He kept his hand on the valve and his eye on the meter.

"Eddie sure is happy to get this fuel." I said to Donnie, who was twice as big as me.

Donnie looked puzzled but said nothing. After several minutes the pump started whining so he closed the valve.

"How much did he get? I asked.

Donnie looked at me and then pointed at the meter. I took a peak. It registered 192 gallons.

"That doesn't seem like very much." I said.

Donnie finally spoke. "That's more than you think. That should last awhile."

Then Eddie came out and helped Donnie strap the hose down on the truck.

"You need some money?" Eddie asked him. "Hell, what am I saying? I can't pay you. I don't have that kind of money on me."

"That's okay. We can settle up later. Sorry about the delay."

It was a struggle, but Donnie managed to climb back into the cab of his truck. He pulled off the lot and headed west to the bypass to begin his four-hour return trip to southwest Virginia.

"Eddie. Really?" I said. "192 gallons of fuel? A couple race cars could burn that up in a day. That's nothing."

"Steve, you are very observant. Follow me."

I followed Eddie into the shed. On the outside wall was an above ground 270-gallon tank typically used for storing heating oil. Two walls were lined with shelves stacked with cases of empty half-pint, pint, quart and half gallon jars. Another shelf stored hoses, funnels, cheesecloth and bottles of corn syrup and other sweeteners. Against the fourth wall was a refrigerator, a dishwasher and a labeling machine. Eddie opened the refrigerator which was stocked with fresh strawberries and the freezer was filled with boxes of assorted fruits.

"Well you sly bastard. I've never heard of anyone buying moonshine in bulk. And you call it racing fuel."

"You gotta call it something. Everybody has a nickname for it."

"Well, I'm impressed," I said.

"Thanks. It's a pretty lucrative business. As far as I know, I'm the only game in the area."

"I have to ask. What do you pay for that?"

"Since you have to ask, I pay around $30 a gallon."

"Wow! Really? Let's see. You've got six grand tied up in that."

"I know. But I can get $50 to $60 a gallon for it after I bottle it."

"So you can double your money?" I asked.

"Just about."

"I had no idea." I said.

"What?"

I shook my head. "I had no idea you peddled the stuff. I've never seen you deliver it or anyone pick it up."

"I keep it quiet. I don't advertise in the paper. I don't have a drive thru window. By the way, I trust you'll keep a lid on this. Ha Ha."

"Your secret is safe with me," I assured him.

"Cool. I know I can trust you. That's why I showed you the operation. Let's put the car away and get out of here."

Eddie locked the shed and we entered the shop through the rear door. Eddie noticed the red light flashing on the office phone. He found the Chevelle key and handed the ring to me.

"Here. You said you wanted to drive it. Back it into the garage. Aw, hell, drive it around the building a couple times, if you want."

I hustled over to the fourth bay, I punched the garage door button and watched the door slowly rise. I got in the Chevelle, fired it up and drove five laps around the shop. I could see Eddie pacing while talking on the phone each time I passed by the front of the building.

I backed it up in the shop and shut her down. I shifted pretty well for not driving a stick shift for a few years. Eddie walked up and I tossed him the key ring.

"Who were you talking to?" I asked.

"Two guys left messages about ordering some fuel. So I called them back. Also, there was a message from the sheriff to call him back. He said they locked up Luis again. He said he would let him go in the morning so there wouldn't be no more trouble tonight."

"Any more trouble." I interjected without thinking.

"What?" Eddie said puzzled.

"Sorry. I can't help it."

"Help what?"

"The double negative."

"Double what?"

"Your sentence had the word 'no' in it twice. That's called a double negative.

Eddie looked at me like I was a jackass. I felt like a jackass.

"Sorry man," I said. "I can't help it."

I needed to change the subject, so I said, "Let's get out of here. We have a race to watch."

14

Eddie shoved his hat on his head, grabbed his cooler, opened it up and took an inventory. He looked disappointed. I helped him put the cloth cover back on the Chevelle. He reloaded the cooler from his refrigerator near the office, and then locked the garage as we exited the front door. We got in my Bronco and looked at each other. However this time Eddie knew where he wanted to go.

"Have you been to Benny's?" Eddie asked.

"Nope. I've been to Ben and Jerrys."

"That's real funny. First you're an English Professor and now you're a comedian. Benny's is a small pool hall downtown. It's in the basement of an old building on Indian Alley."

"That sounds pretty cool." I said.

"It is. It has four full-size pool tables and only two TVs. The only negative thing is they only sell beer."

"Is that where we're watching the race?" I asked.

"Yep. The owner happens to be my bookie."

"Sounds good to me. Maybe it will be quiet down there. Maybe we'll be inconspicuous for a change. I haven't paid much attention to the race this year. I don't know one horse that's running. All I know is that the Derby always has a big field."

"Benny should have a racing form."

"Which way? I asked.

"Good question. It is smack downtown. Hell, go right. We'll try to park near Blivs. I'm sure you'll want to go in there sometime tonight."

"Probably." I said.

I pulled out onto Fairmont Avenue and only drove thirty yards before slowing down to a crawl.

"Check this out."

I put a homemade CD of various Steve Earle songs in the player and forwarded it to "Six Days On The Road."

"I love this song," Eddie yelled. "Turn it up. I need a beer. You?"

"Sure. At this pace, it will probably take a half hour to get downtown."

Eddie popped open two Busch Light beers. "Start the damn song over." Eddie demanded. I did. We both belted out the song as loud as we could sing while rolling along at two miles an hour.

Well, I pulled out of Pittsburgh,
Rollin' down the Eastern Seaboard.
I've got my diesel wound up,
And she's running like never before.
There's a speed zone ahead, all right,
I don't see a cop in sight.
Six days on the road and I'm gonna make it home tonight.

"Are you going to make it home tonight?" I asked.
"I'd like to. But as crazy as this weekend has been so far, who knows?"

The traffic was increasing and the streets were crowded with jaywalkers. We came to a standstill. People were darting around us in both directions. It was like a swarm of insects pestering us. The song ended and I turned down the volume.

"Hey Eddie. I've been thinking and trying to piece this thing together."

"What thing?"

"The whole Lily thing. I wish I could figure out what happened."

"You and me both."

We both sat there quietly, thinking. Pedestrians were making better time than we were. I was glad I had an automatic transmission. I fast forwarded the CD to "Continental Trailways Blues" and turned up the volume.

Well, sittin' in the depot long before the break of day.
I just bought my ticket, Lord I hope the bus ain't late.
I'll have a cup of coffee and a sandwich from the microwave.
Now I'm gonna see my baby if it's the last thing I ever do.
Got this sittin' in the station sick and tired of waitin'
Continental Trailways blues

"You ever take the bus on a long trip?" Eddie asked.

"Once, but not on purpose."

Eddie looked confused.

"I went to the Peach Bowl in Atlanta back in the late 70s. I wrecked my car about an hour before the game. I could see Fulton County Stadium from the wreck."

"What happened?" Eddie seemed interested.

"I rear-ended a car that rear-ended the car in front of it. Anyway, it needed some body work done so my buddies and me took the bus home. Took about eighteen hours. Stopped in every frickin town and we had a long layover in Charlotte. It was miserable."

"That sucks." Eddie said.

"It would be good to get out of town. Way out of town I mean."

"I hear you." Eddie said.

"Speaking of out of town, you said you had to leave town Thursday to run an errand."

"Yeah. That's right."

"Do you mind telling me where you went? I'm just trying to piece everything together. Figure out what happened."

"I don't mind telling you, but this is between you and me. Okay?"

"Sure man. Between you and me."

"On Wednesday," Eddie began slowly, " some guy named Nick left a message on the office phone. On my separate number for the racing fuel orders. Anyway, Skull jotted down the order which was for 15 gallons, in quart jars, to be delivered in Martinsburg. That's a huge order for me and a lot of money for running up there and back. A couple problems, though. It pretty much wiped out my inventory and I don't know the guy. I was a little nervous about it but I figured he got my number from another customer of mine.

Anyway, I get there and I'm sittin' in the parking lot waiting for this guy to show up. I sat there 45 minutes, maybe longer, and no one shows. So I came back to town and drove straight to the bowling alley. And that's why I was late."

"So you have nobody to verify your alibi." I interrupted.

"That's right. Convenient, huh?" Eddie said, half smiling.

"What do you mean?" I asked.

"I think I was sent on a wild goose chase," Eddie said as if it should have been obvious.

"If you're right, someone called, placed an order, and had no intention of picking it up. They just wanted to get you out of town."

"That's the way I got it figured," Eddie said.

"You may be right. But who would have done that?"

"Hell if I know. Who poisoned Lily? Who wrote me that note? Who entered the shop? Who slashed my tires? Who contacted that prick realtor?"

Eddie crushed his can. "You let me know when you figure it out."

"Hey, there's a parking spot opening up." I blurted out.

Great luck. A family of five in a 1983 monkey-shit brown Dodge Dart was fleeing the scene. I parallel parked with ease. We were a little farther out than desired, but on this weekend, you take what you can get. On the west side of town, the sun was dropping behind the city buildings making long shadows and decreasing the temperature.

We walked down the middle of a side street heading toward Berkeley Avenue. The residents, hanging out and drinking on their porches, cheered as we walked by. Eddie pretended to moon one group of them. At Berkeley we headed toward town and walked past the fire hydrant that Eddie had blocked last night. Today it was blocked by a festival golf cart. At the corner of Piccadilly St., I took a look toward O'Blivions.

"Not yet," Eddie said. "She'll be there all night."

"I know. Besides we need to place some bets."

The rest of our walk was pretty uneventful. The parade had most likely ended. People were heading away from the parade route and making tracks for the carnival, the circus, restaurants, and home. Parents were pushing strollers full of souvenirs while carrying their exhausted children. Dogs on leashes were anxious to leave.

We lumbered past the fire station and turned south on Indian Alley. There were few people about since only the locals know about the alley. On the next corner we arrived at Benny's. According to Eddie, of all the businesses in town affected by Apple Blossom, Benny's is probably affected the least. In other words, the clientele doesn't change much. I stared down the long, narrow stairwell. This place was definitely handicap inaccessible. We walked down the stairs and rang the buzzer. Someone buzzed us back and we entered.

The room was dimly lit, smoky as hell, but fairly quiet for the crowd. Twelve bar stools accompanied the bar that ran along the left wall. Every stool was occupied by men with three day beards, smoking and drinking cans of beer. No men were dressed in bright green Dockers slacks and pink Ralph Lauren long-sleeve shirts. No ladies were wearing cherry red Ann Taylor dresses with large black hats. It was damn near 5:45 and the TV in the corner was airing the pre-race coverage.

At the far end of the bar sat a jar of pickled eggs and an elderly, overweight, white haired gentleman. His suspenders were stretched to the max. He wore a green visor and chewed on a short stogie. I followed Eddie to the end of the bar.

"Eddie, it's been awhile." Benny said.

"How you been, Benny?"

"Not bad. Apple blossom is a pain in the ass. You know."

"This is Steve Larkin."

Benny extended his arm and I shook his short, stubby fingered hand. Eddie held up two fingers and Benny got the hint. He retrieved two cans of Busch from the cooler. Eddie leaned toward Benny and lowered his voice.

"We want to put a couple bets down. Let me see your racing form?"

"I had one, but somebody lifted it. I guess they needed it more than I do. There's a paper over there."

"Well, shit. I need some inside information." Eddie said, disappointed. "So Benny, what's the inside scoop? You got any hot tips? I know the Derby is hard to pick since it has such a big field."

"Yeah, I got some tips," Benny said, scratching his head. "Let's see, now. Eighteen horses are going off. The sky is overcast and the track is fast. A. P. Indy scratched. The big favorite is Arazi, some horse from Europe. Dance Floor is supposed to run well. He's owned by some musician named Hammer."

"MC Hammer?" I interrupted.

"I don't know. How many Hammers are there?" Benny said. "Another horse that people are talking about is Casual Lies."

Someone yelled for a beer so Benny walked off toward the other end of the bar. I looked at Eddie.

"Grab that paper. I want to see the whole field. I like to bet on the jockeys anyway."

"That's not a bad idea," Eddie said as he handed me the paper which was already turned to the sports page.

"Let's see here, Jerry Bailey is damn good. He's riding Technology. Gary Stevens is on Casual Lies.

Eddie said "Who's Pat Day riding?"

I scrolled down. "Lil E Tee."

"Who?" Eddie's head spun around.

"Lil E Tee." I repeated.

"Let me see that." Eddie grabbed the paper away from me.

"Son-of-a-bitch," he said slowly.

"What?"

"Lil E Tee. As in Lily Tavarez!" Eddie said, as if I should have made the connection.

"Now I get it. What are the odds?" I asked.

Eddie glanced at the paper. "17:1."

We looked at each other and then at the TV. The horses were leaving the paddock and heading toward the starting gate.

"Benny, come here," Eddie said impatiently.

Benny waddled toward us and eventually arrived.

"A hundred bucks, Lil E Tee on the nose," Eddie said.

Eddie looked at me. "You?".

I looked at Benny. "Twenty bucks."

"Same pony?" He asked.

"Same pony," I confirmed.

"On the nose?"

I looked at Eddie. He was nodding.

"On the nose." I yelled a little too loudly.

Benny turned around, parted two curtains, and disappeared into the back room.

I looked back at Eddie. "What did I just bet on?"

"You took a long shot to win." Eddie said.

"Yikes!" I said.

Eddie and I were glued to the TV. The analysts were taking turns highlighting each horse as they made their way toward the starting gate. Eventually they focused on Lil E Tee.

The narrator's voice said, "This beautiful chestnut brown horse hails from Arkansas. It underwent lifesaving stomach surgery as a yearling, dimming his racing prospects. But here he is today racing in the greatest horse race in the world. He's medium sized compared to the other horses and appears a bit nervous. I can't blame him. Pat Day, sporting an orange polka dot jersey, is rubbing his neck trying to calm him down as they enter the tenth gate. He's going off at odds of 17:1."

Benny appeared out of nowhere and turned up the volume on the TV. Eddie stuck up two fingers. As the last horse entered the last gate, the pool games came to a sudden halt and everyone at the bar turned toward the TV.

"Here we go!" Eddie yelled.

The bell rang, the gates flew open and the TV analyst yelled "And they're off."

15

Lil E Tee broke sharply, but quickly got swallowed up by the pack. By the quarter turn, Snappy Landing and Devil His Due were leading. By the halfway mark, Casual Lies, Dance Floor and Pine Bluff were running first, second and third. Lil E Tee had fallen to next to last.

"Come on Lily." I yelled at the TV.

"Be patient," Eddie said calmly.

Then, Pat Day, sporting the orange polka dot jersey, began to weave his horse through the pack. By the middle of the third turn, Lil E Tee had moved into seventh place directly behind Arazi. Then, Arazi charged to the outside and Lil E Tee quickly followed. Arazi blew past three horses and at this point Pat Day would later say "I figured I was racing for second place." However, at the start of the backstretch Arazi began to run out of steam.

Eddie grabbed my arm as he stood up. "He's fading. He's fading. Go back to steeple chase you European jackass."

As the horses came down the backstretch, everyone in the bar was yelling and cheering for their horse. Arazi moved off the outside toward the rail and Lil E Tee flew by him. He was running strong but still had some ground to make up. Dance Floor and Casual Lies were battling for first place. With a hundred yards to go, Lil E Tee was closing the gap on the outside.

Eddie squeezed my arm a little harder. "Come on. Come on." He yelled a little louder each time. Pat Day pounded Lil E Tee with the whip like there was no tomorrow. Eddie was making a whipping motion with his right hand against his right hip as if he was in the race.

"Come on dammit!.... Do it for Lily." Eddie yelled.

At this moment, I convinced myself there was no way that Eddie had intentionally taken Liliana Tavarez's life.

Lil E Tee passed Casual Ties with thirty yards to go and went on to win by one length. The race took two minutes and three seconds, one of the slowest races in recent Derby history. Lil E Tee never received the recognition he deserved for winning. Instead, critics blamed Arazi for losing the race that was his to win.

Eddie leaped into the air with his fist raised. If the ceiling fan had been any lower, he would have punched it. "Yes.... We did it." He screamed.

We hugged each other and danced around in circles. A couple of other people got excited, as if they had won something, but nobody was as jacked as we were. Eventually everyone in the pool hall had their eyes on us. They knew we had won big and were expecting a free beer at some point. We returned to our stools.

"How much did we win?" I whispered in Eddie's ear.

"17 to 1 times twenty bucks is $340."

"Wow! What's your payout?" I said without doing the math.

"About $1,700. Not bad for a two-minute race."

Back on the TV, Lil E Tee was receiving the bed of roses in the winner's circle. The owner and trainer appeared to be as surprised to have won as Eddie and I were. Benny reappeared through the curtains from the back room carrying a couple of envelopes. He waddled down to the other end of the bar and handed them to two scruffy looking guys drinking Red Dog. He walked back up to us empty handed.

"Nice job, guys. And to think you came in here asking me for a tip. I should have asked you guys for a tip."

"Sometimes it pays to bet on the jockey," Eddie said, trying to keep from laughing. "Can you cover our bets?"

"Yeah. I got it in the safe," Benny said proudly.

"Cool. Pay Steve here and just give me $500. I'll collect the rest next week."

"You got it."

Benny parted the curtains and disappeared.

1992 Kentucky Derby Results

	WIN	PLACE	SHOW
Lil E. Tee	$35.60	$12.20	$7.60
Casual Lies		$22.00	$11.60
Dance Floor			$12.60

We looked back up at the TV just as the replay of the race was about to start.

"Hey, Eddie. Did I ever tell you about my idea to breed jockeys?"

"No. Breed what?" Eddie said as he took a swig off of his beer.

"Yeah. I got this idea one night. You know how they put race horses out to stud after their racing career is over."

"Yeah," Eddie said. I was getting his attention.

"Well, I had this idea that when jockeys get too old to race, you put them out to stud, too."

"Go on." Eddie said.

"Yeah. You put the jockey out in a pasture. You give him some patio furniture with an umbrella. Give him a cooler, a couple sandwiches and some magazines. You know. Make him comfortable."

"Continue." Eddie was smiling.

"Then you release some small women into the pasture. Hopefully they turn him on and he knocks them up. A few years later, you should be able to tell whether or not the offspring will be small enough to become a jockey."

"Steve.... That's brilliant. Do you think any women's rights groups will object?"

"Probably all of them."

"Maybe we should contact Willie Shoemaker. He's retired." Eddie suggested.

Benny returned from the back and handed each of us an envelope. Eddie removed $50 from his and handed it to Benny.

"Here. Set up the bar. And get yourself something."

"Will do." Benny said.

"See you next week, Benny. Finish your beer Steve, we've got places to go."

I pretended to chug my beer. We slipped out the front door and climbed the stairs. The bar had been so dark, I forgot that it was still daylight outside.

"Now what?" I asked. I was feeling pretty good. I had a good beer buzz going and I was $340 richer.

"What do you say we stroll through the carnival. Check out all the derelicts," Eddie said.

"Sure. I'm up for anything."

We popped out on the alley and walked back up to the fire station. The garage doors were open exposing the fire trucks to the general public. Eddie shot the shit with some of the firemen for about twenty minutes. Then we headed east on Boscawen, turned north at Cameron, crossed Piccadilly and entered the carnival on the south side.

By now dusk was setting in and it became noticeable that the temperature had dropped. I always thought carnivals were more tolerable at night than in the daylight. Tonight the carnival had the typical crowd, sounds and odors.

Teenage boys, sporting sleeveless Guns N Roses t-shirts, holding hands with even younger girls, were crying out to be noticed. Distorted Top 40 music blared through worn out speakers from each ride. Kids, on rides, were screaming from joy and fear. The stagnant air was saturated with a blended smell of sausages, funnel cakes, cigarettes and burnt oil.

"Oh shit." Eddie blurted out. "Look who's walkin toward us."

"Who?" I asked.

"Hang on. Hey, Frank. How you doin?" Eddie said, insincerely.

"Well if it isn't Eddie Robinson," Frank said as he held out his hand.

"What brings you guys to the carnival?" He asked.

"Ah, you know. We're here for the great music and gourmet food. This here is Steve Larkin."

"Howdy, Steve," Frank said.

"Frank, what's different about you? Haircut?" Eddie asked.

"I lost my glasses a couple days ago. The damndest thing. They just disappeared. I waited until today to try and get a new pair and of course the stores are closed. Apple Blossom and all. Anyway, I have an old pair of contacts in."

"Frank, I hate to cut this short, but Steve and I gotta go see a man about a dog. Later." Eddie said in a hurry.

We walked off and I asked. "Who was that?"

"Frank Reynolds. He's a big shot banker in town. He's full of himself. A solid asshole. As your good friend R. Satterfield would say: "He couldn't hit a bull in the ass with a banjo." Oh, and he lives in that house on Washington Street where I ran up and yelled at that real estate prick today."

"Did you say Frank Reynolds?"

"Yeah. Why?"

"Nothin'. That name rings a bell."

Eddie broke into a trot and once again I had trouble keeping up with him. He slowed down a bit when we approached the galleries. Some free entertainment waited ahead of us.

Fathers and sons were shooting BB guns with bent sights at paper targets, old women were tossing nickels at glass plates and bowls, boyfriends were whaling darts at balloons in hopes of winning large stuffed animals for their girlfriends, and little kids were picking up floating ducks for a guaranteed prize.

After walking the circuit, we arrived at the midway. People of all ages were waiting in long lines to board the Merry-Go-Round, the Tea Cup and The Whip. Eventually, we walked up on the Gravitron and I recognized the operator.

"Hey, look. It's Scrambler."

"Who?" Eddie asked.

"Scrambler. Remember? From Patricks?"

Eddie looked unimpressed as he placed a dip between his cheek and gum. Scrambler was wearing the same clothes as yesterday with the exception of a solid red bandana on his head. He had his right hand on the throttle and a 20-ounce plastic bottle of Mountain Dew in his back pocket. I leaned over the railing and tapped him on the shoulder.

"Hey, man. Remember us?" I shouted over the noisy engine.

He hesitated and then smiled. "Yeah. You bought me a beer yesterday."

"You got your job back," I yelled.

"Yeah. Hold on a second." He backed the throttle off and the ride started to slow down. "They begged me to come back. I guess they need me more than I need them. They put me on this Gravitron ride. It's okay. It's different."

Eddie looked restless.

"We'll let you go, man. You're busy," I said.

"I got about three more hours," he said. "Then it's Miller time." He looked up in the air. "Man, it's getting cold."

I looked up, too, but the lights and smoke were unwilling to reveal the emerging stars.

"Hey, come over to O'Blivions later. I'll buy you some High Lifes. It's on Piccadilly Street."

"Really? Thanks, man. Hey you guys watch out. There is some trouble brewing."

"What do you mean?" I asked.

"There's a couple Mexican gangs here that are acting kind a strange."

Eddie spun around.

"I haven't worked the carnival long, but I can tell when something is about to go down.

16

"Let's get out of here." I suggested.

"I'm tempted to stick around but you're smarter than me. Let's go, professor." Eddie said.

We hurried passed the food vendors and took in the aromas of Italian sausages, corn on the cob and kettle korn. It smelled good for a brief moment. We exited the carnival on the west side and popped out on Race Street.

"Where to?" We both said at the same time.

"I know where you want to go," Eddie said with a shit-eating grin.

"Well, we are close. Besides I want to check on the Pirate game."

"What do you say first we walk up to the shop and let me take a quick shower and change of clothes."

"Sure. It's early," I answered.

The stars were out and the cold air contributed to us walking at a pretty good clip. We could smell the apple juice plant long before we reached it.

"Does Art sell fruit to this plant?" I asked.

"Sure. Everybody does. They don't want to, but they do."

"Why's that?"

"Cause the prices are shitty. You only get about $8 per hundred weight. Or about $3 per bushel."

"That's awful." I said.

"Tell me about it. Prices were higher twenty, even thirty years ago than they are today. Back then, growers planted processing varieties such as Rome Beauty and York Imperial because the prices were good. A lot of those processing varieties aren't fit to eat so you have to sauce or juice them. The plant also buys the rejects from the packing houses. They set their prices in early summer and then the growers are at their mercy."

"So how do they determine the price?" I asked to make small talk.

"It's based on the estimate for this year's crop and the inventory left over from last year's crop. If the crop in the region is big, they don't hardly pay you anything. If the crop is small, they pay you more but you don't have a big crop. It's a lose, lose situation."

We reached the shop's dimly lit parking lot. Eddie's Suburban was still leaning to the left. We entered the front door. Eddie threw on some lights, punched the radio and disappeared behind the office. A George Strait song aroused Rocket. He was annoyed by our appearance after dark. I heard the shower come on.

I walked through the shop searching for clues. I looked for notes and clues by the phone. I looked for a door leading from the shop to the moonshine room but couldn't find one. I eventually ended up at the fourth bay and pulled the cover off the Chevelle. Did Eddie drive it out to the cabin? Did someone get the key off of Eddie's key ring? Was there another key that Eddie didn't know about? Did someone else in town drive a sports car with the same tire tread as the Chevelle? I was asking myself these questions when Eddie appeared buttoning up a dark green long-sleeved shirt.

"What are you doing?" Eddie asked politely.

"I was just looking to see if I left anything in the car," I tried to say sincerely.

"Did you?"

"No. You ready?"

"Not quite. The light is blinking on the phone."

"Racing fuel orders?" I asked while replacing the cover.

"Probably, but I better check it out."

Eddie held the phone up to his ear and punched in some numbers. I piddled around the shop trying to eaves drop. He only made one call and told some one that he could take care of them on Monday.

"Let's get out of here, you want a jacket?" Eddie yelled.

"That's not a bad idea. It's getting colder by the minute. Should you try to get a hold of Skull?"

"Nah. I think she went to her mother's place for the weekend. Hey, you want a shot of white lightning?"

"Normally, I would say 'no thanks,' but tonight...what the hell." I said.

"That's the spirit."

Eddie went back to the office area and returned with two jackets. One was a blue shop jacket with the Eddie's Garage logo and the other was a heavy red flannel shirt.

"Take your pick," Eddie said while holding them up.

"Tough decision. Give me the red one. Thanks."

We covered the car and Eddie killed most of the lights as we slipped out the rear door. We walked over to the moonshine shed and Eddie unlocked the door. I was even more impressed this time than earlier in the day. The assembly line was very well thought out.

"What flavor ol' buddy?" Eddie asked me.

"Surprise me."

"You like it cold or warm?"

I had to think for a few seconds. "Cold."

Eddie went to the refrigerator and opened the crisper drawer. He removed a pint jar and held it up to the light.

"Look here, Steve, canary-piss yellow."

He unscrewed the lid and handed it to me. "Try that," he said as he winked at me.

Moonshine scares the hell out of me so I just took a sip. I started to hand it back to him when it hit me how good it was.

"Pineapple?" I asked.

"You know it. Pretty good, huh?"

"That's amazingly smooth."

This time I took a swig from the jar and handed it back to Eddie. He took a healthy swallow and screwed the lid back on.

"We should take this downtown," Eddie said. "We may run into somebody downtown who wants a quality shot."

"Speaking of downtown, let's go," I suggested.

Eddie locked up the liquor store, put in a big dip, and we headed toward town. We walked up on the juice plant and Eddie said, "Come on. Let's check out the bins."

We walked to the side of the lot where the street light illuminated thousands of empty bins. They ranged in size from eighteen bushels to twenty-five bushels. Before I knew it, Eddie was taking a leak so I joined him. We zipped up and Eddie said.

"Steve. Look here."

"What?"

Eddie pointed out stacks of bins as we walked along. "Rinker Orchards, they're in Stephen City. H. F. and T. B. Byrd, they're down in Timberville. Marker-Miller Orchards, they're local. Lewis Brothers, they're up in West Virginia. Ayers Orchards, I think they're down around Roanoke. Look here. Pioneer Orchards. We know where they are."

"Art must have two hundred bins here." I said.

"Probably. He's got all summer to haul them back to the bin shed. He won't pick anything until September."

We started walking toward the bright lights of town again. The top of the Ferris Wheel was barely visible. As we walked along, fewer people were partying outside as the temperature continued to drop. Eventually we could hear the carnival which led to smelling it. When we reached Piccadilly Street we turned right. Some people were anxious to get to the carnival while others were fleeing. We walked two more blocks and entered O'Blivions.

17

The place was hopping again. Only this time I recognized more people. The crowd was buzzed and the band was rocking.

"Hey Judd. How's it going?" Eddie asked.

"Huh?" Judd yelled.

"How's it going?" Eddie yelled back.

"Not bad. A little loud in here," Judd yelled just as the song ended. He leaned toward Eddie. "I'll do a better job keeping those spics out of here tonight. They blew right passed me last night."

Eddie cringed.

"Who's the band?" I interjected. Judd turned his attention toward me.

" The Droolers. A SKA band from down around Front Royal."

"That's cool," I said, while realizing the horn section included a trumpet, a trombone a tenor sax and an alto sax.

"Most of their songs are about drinking, getting belligerent and broken hearts. Impressed?" Judd asked.

"Not yet," I said. "But it's early."

We were almost to the bar when I noticed Lisa and Pete hanging out near the stage. She was a very attractive young lady whom I took out a few times when I first moved to town. She was tall, bright, and held a good job at the hospital. But I knew it would never work out, and ended our relationship, after discovering she was a Phillies fan. She looked particularly good this evening. Pete on the other hand was short, stocky and uncoordinated. I nicknamed him "Banjo Head" for the five hairs he combs over his bald head.

We walked to the end of the bar where it wasn't so loud, and just like last night, our beers and a spit cup were waiting for us.

"Hey, guys!" Kelly yelled jumping up and down.

"Hey, Darlin," I said, watching her jump up and down. Tonight she wore pink shorts and a black "Droolers" tee shirt tied in a knot just above her belly button.

"Steve, where have you guys been? Look." She held up a pitcher with the flowers that I had dropped off earlier in the day.

"These are awesome.....Iris right?"

"That's right." She leaned over the bar as much as she could and gave me a hug.

"Let me run a tab. We'll probably be here for awhile..... Busy, huh?"

"Yeah, but there's four of us. We can handle it." She said.

"By the way, you really look hot tonight." I said.

"Thanks. I was hoping you would say something."

She motioned for both of us to lean toward her. "Some guy called here about an hour and a half ago and asked for Eddie. I told him Eddie wasn't here and the guy says 'When he gets there, tell him to wait for me'."

"I asked who it was, but he hung up on me."

Eddie looked over his shoulder then chugged his beer.

I said, "Did you recognize the voice?"

"No," Kelly said.

"Did he sound Hispanic?'

"No. Should he have?"

Eddie and I looked at each other and then back at Kelly. He ordered two Mint Juleps.

"Don't worry about it," I told Eddie.

Kelly returned with the drinks. Eddie thanked her with a nod, handed me a drink and said, "Cheers!" He walked off toward the dart lanes.

"Hey Kelly, can you switch the TV to ESPN? The Pirates and Astros should be the Saturday night game of the week."

"Anything for you baby." She switched the channel just as the Pirates made the last out in the top of the seventh inning. Pirates 6 - Astros 0. Kelly ran off to wait on some impatient customers.

"Awesome," I said to myself. "It should be difficult for the Astros to overcome a six-run deficit." I scanned the room while taking in the band. The horn section sounded crisp and refreshing.

One dude had his head on the table but both hands were wrapped tightly around his beer bottle. Three braless hippie chicks were swinging everything they had in front of the stage. Two older couples, dressed in the official Apple Blossom attire, were sprawled out at a table sipping brandy.

Three of the four dart lanes were taken up by amateurs. It was pretty obvious. One group put their wrong foot forward when they threw, another group was playing cricket, no points and the third group was playing a game of baseball. The far lane was occupied by Eddie and Clint Sturgill. Clint was a member of our dart team and a damn good 501 player.

Back at the TV, the Astros were coming to bat. In a brief inning, it was three up and three down. 'On to the eighth'. I said to myself. The other TV was showing Kentucky Derby highlights. It still amazed me how Lil E Tee managed to blow his way through the field like he did. Two guys walked up beside me.

"Some race huh?"

I turned to my right. It was Mason from the greenhouse. We worked together occasionally. Anytime I had a lab in the greenhouse, he would help me set it up. He earned a degree in horticulture back in the mid 70s when the major was sexier than it is today. His long pony tail backs up his claim that he hasn't had a haircut since he graduated. He hails from Loudoun County which is horse country.

"Hey, Mason. What's going on?" I didn't wait for an answer. "One hell of a race."

"Sure was." He said disappointedly while scratching his head. "I had Casual Lies to win. He was looking great until that long shot prick passed him at the end."

"Yeah. I saw that." I said. "Who's your sidekick?"

"Oh, sorry. Where are my manners? I'm still depressed about the race. This is Kenny Patterson."

"Hey, Kenny, I'm Steve." We shook hands. "Let me buy you guys a drink."

"What are you drinking?" Mason asked.

"Mint Julep. The official drink of the Kentucky Derby. Let's see. It's bourbon, sugar water, and crushed mint leaves. You guys want one?"

"Why not?" Mason said. "Okay with you, Kenny?"

Kenny nodded.

I looked down the bar and found Kelly staring at me. I held up two fingers and pointed at my glass. I watched her make the drinks which aren't complicated except for mashing the mint leaves with a mortar and pestle. She returned with the drinks and a big smile. I handed them out as I watched her walk away.

"Thanks," Mason said. "Yeah. Thanks," Kenny chimed in.

"Here's to Apple Blossom," I yelled while lifting my glass. Several more people heard me and joined in on the toast.

"What do you do Kenny?" I asked.

"I'm one of the service managers at General Motors. I help people with restorations. "

"Is that right? Do you have a card?"

"I should. What do you drive? Don't tell me. I like to guess." He looked me up and down as he was searching his wallet for a card. "Buick? No." He quickly changed his mind. "You look more like a truck guy. Silverado? No. You look like an SUV guy. Suburban? I'm sticking with Suburban."

"My buddy drives a Suburban. I drive a Bronco," I said proudly.

"Never would have guessed that. Here's my card. Why do you want my card anyway?"

"I might need some advice sometime."

I stuck the card in my shirt pocket.

"Mason, you want to mosey around?" Kenny asked.

"Sure. Thanks for the drink," they both said and walked off.

I returned to the TV only to find out I missed the entire eighth inning. The Pirates were coming to bat in the top of the 9th still leading 6 to 0. I waved at a couple guys I know at the end of the bar. Kelly returned and handed me a beer and a bowl of Chex mix.

"I figured you'd need another beer sooner or later."

"Thanks, sweetie."

"How's the Mint Julep?" she asked.

"It's okay. I'm nursing it."

"Where is Eddie? Is he throwing darts?" she asked. We both looked over at the dart lanes. Eddie and Clint were still shooting the shit in lane four.

"The only thing Eddie is throwing is moonshine down his throat."

"Have him save me a sip," Kelly said as she walked off.

"If there's any left," I yelled behind her.

The band announced that since they had already consumed a case of beer, they needed to take a break after one more song to drain their horns. The Pirates had two outs but were still in good shape. I looked toward the door and Judd was carding a young man. When he turned toward the bar, I recognized him.

"Scrambler. Over here," I yelled.

He couldn't hear me over the band but my waving arms caught his eye. He weaved through the crowd and arrived at the bar just as Eddie and Clint did too.

"Scrambler, my man." I hugged his shoulder. "Do you want a High Life or a shot?"

"Sure," he said.

"Good answer," I said. "Hey, Eddie, you got anything left in the jar?"

"Yeah. You want some?"

"No, but Kelly does."

"Here. She can have the rest." He said while handing it to me.

I motioned for her to come back our way and showed her the pint jar.

"I'll give this to you later. In the meantime, get Scrambler here a High Life and a Mint Julep on me."

"Clint, how you been ol' buddy?" I asked.

"Not bad. Are you throwin' darts this summer?"

"I don't know. I'm planning to travel some and fish a lot. So I may just be a sub. If that's okay."

"It's okay with me. You know how the summer leagues are. Everyone's on the go."

The Astros were coming to bat in the bottom of the ninth. Eddie let out a double sneeze. I kept chatting with Clint and Scrambler and watching the game. Eddie sneezed three more times with his head lowered to the floor. He came up and I handed him a napkin.

"One out," I yelled out loud.

Eddie bent over for four more sneezes. Someone out of nowhere said 'Bless You' after his ninth sneeze. Who waits for nine sneezes before saying Bless You? I thought to myself. Personally, I don't bless anybody or anything. Eddie rose up slowly as if he was finished and then bent over quickly for two more.

"What's your record?" I yelled down at him.

He rose up and said "Seventeen."

I pushed his head back toward the floor. "You have a long way to go pal."

"Two outs," I yelled. No one else seemed to care. Scrambler was standing there double fisted.

"How's that Mint Julep Scrambler?"

He nodded as if he was enjoying it.

Eddie sneezed two more times but the interval between sneezes was increasing. I decided to fuck with Eddie a little. I grabbed a pepper shaker off the bar and shook it over his head. Clint and Scrambler were howling. Eddie sneezed two more times but it was coming to an end. The pepper probably had no effect and Eddie finally stood up.

"Fifteen?" I asked.

Eddie nodded.

"A gallant effort," I said. I started clapping and several other people joined in. Eddie shook his head like a dog leaving a lake.

The band was returning to the stage and I returned to the TV. The Astros had runners on first and second when Jeff Bagwell grounded out to end the game. I pumped my fist. Bonds and Van Slyke combined for 5 of the 6 RBIs and Neagle earned his first win of the year.

Kelly saw me celebrating and came down to our end of the bar. I put my hand on her hand.

"I'm buying a round. You guys want beers this time?"

Everyone was ready to switch back to beer.

"Get Scrambler a High Life. Get Eddie the shittiest beer you have. And get two Bass Ales for Clint and me."

"You got it," She said.

I think all of us watched her walk away. Then we turned toward the band. The horn section took turns belting out solos. Kelly returned with our beers and handed Eddie an Old Milwaukee Tall Boy.

"Where did you find that?" I asked, laughing.

"I had to dig deep in the cooler. Hard to tell how old it is." She said, smiling.

Eddie got excited. "I haven't had one of these in years. Thanks."

We toasted to baseball, horses, apple blossoms and good looking broads. Eddie made some strange faces after drinking from his can. After all the toasting we were empty again.

"Another round?" I offered.

Scrambler said "I got to get to work early tomorrow. We got to tear everything down. I think we're heading to Baltimore."

"Okay, buddy. You take care." I said.

"See you guys next year," Scrambler said before walking away.

Eddie and I looked at each other.

"We're supposed to be fishing," Eddie said sadly.

"I know. Oh, are you going to wait for that guy who called the bar looking for you?" I asked.

"That was Clint here. He wanted to talk about the dart league party next week." Clint smiled.

"What do you guys want to do?" I asked.

"I don't know. How bout you?" Eddie asked me.

"Since our horse won and the Pirates won, I'd like to engage in some Victory Sex."

"Don't look at me." Eddie said.

"Victory Sex? What's that?" Kelly said as she popped up from behind the bar.

"Yeah. What in the hell is Victory Sex?" Clint asked.

I looked at all three of them. "It's like normal sex except there are a lot of high fives going on."

There are many stories about the origin of the high five but the most documented candidates are Dusty Baker and Glenn Burke of the Los Angeles Dodgers on October 2, 1977.

It was the last day of the regular season, and Dodgers leftfielder Dusty Baker had just gone deep off the Astros' J.R. Richard. It was Baker's 30th home run, making the Dodgers the first team in history to have four sluggers (Baker, Ron Cey, Steve Garvey and Reggie Smith) with at least 30 homers each.

It was a wild, triumphant moment and a good omen as the Dodgers headed to the playoffs. Burke, waiting on deck, thrust his hand enthusiastically over his head to greet his friend at the plate. Baker, not knowing what to do, smacked it. "His hand was up in the air, and he was arching way back," says Baker, "So I reached up and hit his hand. It seemed like the thing to do.

"Kelly, one more round and I'll settle up with you. Get Eddie a Schaefer or a Busch this time. Get Clint whatever he wants."

"Thanks, but I'm good." Clint said. "I gotta run."

"So long. See you next week," Eddie yelled behind him.

Kelly returned with two beers.

"Now what? I asked.

"I'm too tired to head north. Besides I don't have a vehicle."

"Oh, shit. How are you getting home? I asked.

"I'm not. I'll just crash at the shop again. We gotta meet the sheriff at 10:00. I won't be late."

Eddie drank about half of his beer and set it on the bar. He put a ten spot in the tip jar, waved good-bye and left. Outside he turned right which was the most direct way to the shop. Kelly brought me my tab.

"Victory Sex sounds pretty exciting. You've done that before, have you?" Kelly asked.

"No. I've just heard about it." I said sadly. "I'd like to try it sometime though."

"How about tonight?" Kelly suggested.

"Really?" I asked.

"If you want to. I don't want to impose."

"I want to," I said without having to think about it.

"I'm guessing the opportunity for Victory Sex doesn't come around very often," Kelly said smiling.

"You're right. We better take advantage of it while we can."

I handed Kelly the moonshine. She winked at me and took off toward the kitchen. The band announced that they were going to play a couple more songs. The next song was from the Mighty Mighty Bosstones second album. The song was called "I'll Drink To That." Kelly returned with a beer for me and a plastic cup of Eddie's moonshine for her.

"Travis said I could leave early since I closed last night."

"Great. Tell Travis I owe him one."

"Where do you want to go?" Kelly asked.

"We can go to my place but I've had too many to drive. Besides, my vehicle is parked in the wrong direction. It's pretty cold to walk it. Do you want to drive your car to my place?" I asked.

"I would but I hit a curb Thursday and now I have a flat tire. I may have to change the wheel. Let's go to my place. I live right around the corner. Let me collect my tips and my flowers and we'll get out of here."

"I'll drink to *that*." I said.

May 2nd Starting Lineups

Pittsburgh Pirates   **Houston Astros**

1 Orlando Merced 1B   1 Craig Biggio 2B

2 Jay Bell SS   2 Steve Finley CF

3 Andy Van Slyke CF   3 Jeff Bagwell 1B

4 Barry Bonds LF   4 Pete Incaviglia RF

5 Gary Varsho RF   5 Chris Jones LF

6 Steve Buechele 3B   6 Casey Candaele 3B

7 Mike LaValliere C   7 Scott Servais C

8 Jose Lind 2B   8 Andujar Cedeno SS

9 Denny Neagle P   9 Ryan Bowen P

	1	2	3		4	5	6		7	8	9		R	H	E
Pirates	2	1	0		0	0	0		3	0	0		6	8	0
Astros	0	0	0		0	0	0		0	0	0		0	4	0

18

By 8:30, the morning sun had penetrated the bedroom's maroon shear curtains. I awoke with a slight headache and a smile on my face. Kelly was fast asleep and lying on her side. I raised the sheet to get one last look at her gorgeous body before I sat up. I had a lot on my mind.

I got dressed after struggling to find all my clothes and made a pot of coffee. I rounded up Kelly's cordless phone and phone book and placed them on the kitchen table. My first call was to Sheriff Bob Wilkins. Luckily he was in.

"Sheriff, this is Steve Larkin," I said in a low voice.

"Who?"

"It's Steve. I've been hanging out with Eddie Robinson all weekend."

"Oh, yeah? Is he in trouble?"

"No. Well, hell I don't know. I haven't seen him since last night."

"What can I do for you Steve?"

"I have a couple of theories on what happened to Liliana Tavarez."

"Oh, yeah? Do you want to share these theories with me?"

"I do, but at Eddie's place. I'll meet you there at 10:00. Oh, and bring Luis with you. He needs to be there too."

"Alright. See you at 10:00."

The next person I wanted to talk to was Kenny Patterson. His home number wasn't on his business card so I looked it up in the phone book. There were several Pattersons listed, and by mistake, I called his father first, Kenneth Patterson Sr. He straightened me out and gave me the correct number.

"Kenny, this is Steve Larkin. We met last night at O'Blivions. You remember?"

"Yeah. I gave you my card. I didn't think you'd call so soon.

"I have a favor to ask you."

"Go on."

Eddie and I are meeting the sheriff to discuss some scenarios regarding a crime that was committed recently. There is a vehicle, manufactured from Chevrolet that will most likely be linked to the crime. I have a few questions that I want to ask an expert, such as you, in front of the sheriff. Would you be willing to help me out?"

"Yeah, I suppose. When are you meeting, next week?"

"Actually, we're meeting in about an hour. 10:00 at Eddie's Garage and Video. It shouldn't take long. Can you make it?"

"Yeah. I can make it."

"Do you know where it is?" I asked.

"Yeah, the shop with the naked girl calendars."

"Thanks, buddy. See you there."

Next I called Eddie. I had to look up the number for Eddie's Garage and Video. There was no listing for Eddie's Racing Fuel Hotline. Eddie picked up on the eighth ring.

"Steve, is that you?"

"Yeah. Did I wake you up?"

"I reckon you did. What time is it?"

"A little after 9:00. Listen, I think I may have broken the case.

"What case?" Eddie asked.

"You idiot. The case. I want you to call three people and get them to meet you at the shop at 10:00. I know it's short notice."

"Okay. Who?"

"Call Brian Mercer and tell him you are ready to make a deal."

"What?"

"Just tell him. He'll come down. Call Frank, the big shot banker, and tell him you found a piece of his personal property at the shop. Tell him he has to pick it up by 10:00. Then call Skull and tell her you need a ride home. Call your house, her mother's house and all her friends. Don't give up trying until you find her. You got all that?"

"Yeah. Got it."

"Oh, and don't tell anyone that anyone else is going to be at the shop."

"Where did you end up last night?" Eddie asked.

"You may figure it out when you see me. Make those calls, buddy. See you at 10:00."

I hung up and gave a quick prayer that everyone would be reached and show up. The coffee smelled good but unfortunately I don't drink coffee. Love the smell, can't stand the taste. I've actually only consumed two cups in my lifetime. When someone offers me coffee, I say March, 1975, like a recovering alcoholic will say to someone offering them a drink.

I walked into the bedroom and sat on the bed. Kelly rolled over and said

"You're up."

"Yep, and unfortunately I need to leave soon. I have to meet Eddie and the sheriff up at Eddie's place.

"I know. You told me last night."

"That's right. Well, I better go. I made you coffee. "

"Thanks."

"I had an incredible time last night. Did you?" I asked, hoping for a yes.

She lifted her right hand high over her head and I smacked it pretty hard. I gave her a big kiss and walked into the living room where I found Eddie's red jacket that he lent me on the floor and inside out.

I left the apartment and set out in search of my vehicle. Everything looked remarkably different in the daylight. Heavy frost covered the grass of lawns still in the shade. The streets were deserted and eerie quiet. Even the neighborhood dogs were sleeping in. I eventually found Berkeley Avenue and the side street where the Bronco was parked.

I fired it up and reached toward the back seat for my Pirates hat. I drove to the nearest convenient store where I poured myself a big ass fountain Pepsi. The upper right corner of the paper had another blurb about Lily.

Still no leads in the death of a young woman found dead Friday evening near Back Creek off of Nelson's Ridge Road. Anyone with information is encouraged to call the Frederick County Sheriff's Dept.

As I approached the shop, I became increasingly nervous. Even though I felt confident that I had figured the whole thing out, all of my hunches needed to pan out. I parked in front of the garage and found two of the four garage doors open. Rocket gave me a half hearted welcome. Perhaps he knew it was Sunday, his day of rest. Eddie was in the waiting room, lying on the couch, watching a movie.

"What are you watching there, buddy?" I asked.

"The Great Escape. I'm thinkin' I might end up going to jail today."

"Come on. Don't think like that. Looks like I'm the first one here."

"Just you and me pal. Hey, you're wearing the same clothes. You didn't go home last night. You rascal, you stayed with Kelly?"

"You figured it out." I admitted.

"I hope you didn't correct her English during sex."

"What?"

"I can visualize her moaning 'Yeah… Yeah… Yes' And then you butt in, 'Now Kelly, that's a double positive'."

"You're crazy. Did you get a hold of everybody?"

"Yes, and everyone said they would be here."

"Good. Where was Skull?"

"She was home. Go figure. Hey, somebody's here."

Sheriff Wilkins, Deputy Myers, and Luis entered the garage. Eddie and I walked out to greet them. No one shook hands.

"Let's get started," the sheriff said. "First of all, Luis promised to behave himself. Right Luis?"

He nodded.

I butted in. "Sheriff, I invited a few more people to join us. Can you wait a few minutes?"

"I suppose."

Brian and Frank entered the garage asking each other questions.

"What are you doing here?"

"I'm not sure. What are you doing here?"

Both of them became nervous when they caught a glimpse of the sheriff.

Next, Skull parked her light blue Blazer in front of the third garage door and entered the shop twirling her keys. She was dressed in gray sweat pants, a white Crystal Bar tee shirt and flip flops.

"What's going on? she asked.

Eddie jumped in. "The sheriff's department is investigating a possible homicide on Thursday night. And I believe I am one of the suspects.

"Are you serious? What are these other guys doing here?" She asked.

"We're trying to figure out what happened." Eddie assured her.

Finally, Kenny Patterson entered through the front door. Everyone had shown up and Rocket was confused. I announced to the group that the sheriff was conducting an investigation on the death of Liliana Tavarez. And on top of that, I had some questions and hunches of what happened. I motioned for the sheriff to take charge.

"Eddie, we confirmed that one of the molds made at your cabin matched your Suburban."

"Well, I told you that I had been up there."

"Yesterday, after you left the parade in your Chevelle, we made a mold of your tire tracks from the lawn at the high school. They match the tracks we found at your cabin. Did you drive the Chevelle up to the cabin recently?"

"Nope," Eddie said quickly.

"Who else has access to your car?"

"Absolutely nobody. I have the only key and no one has borrowed it," Eddie said confidently.

"Well Eddie, let's add up some facts here. Thursday afternoon, you called Liliana and asked her to come here, to the garage, to clean. Then you were late to bowling Thursday evening. Liliana's body is discovered late Friday afternoon on your property and the cause of death is determined to be from methanol poisoning. Now I did a little research on the fermentation process.

Although methanol is not produced in toxic amounts by fermentation of sugars from grains, two things can happen. First, distillers can add methanol to increase the strength of the product which is very dangerous. Second, the first few ounces of alcohol that drip from the condenser is called the foreshot. The foreshot contains most of the methanol from the mash because methanol vaporizes at a lower temperature than ethanol. Conscientious moonshiners discard the foreshot.

Now, moonshine was discovered on your property and one jar had a very high level of methanol in it."

"You bastard," Luis yelled at Eddie.

"Settle down," I said. I wanted to butt in but decided to let the sheriff continue.

" Eddie, with everything I've just said and the fact that your car was at the cabin and you have the only key, in my opinion is pretty incriminating. I'll give you a chance to speak but first I just want to say that sometimes things just have a way of getting out of hand. Perhaps you two were up at the cabin with good intentions. Maybe you were sippin' on a little moonshine and things began to go wrong. Maybe she became ill, or fell down or had a seizure. I'm not convinced you killed her but perhaps she died accidentally and you are trying to cover it up."

I looked around the room reading body language. Eddie was squirming and about to spout off when I jumped in.

"Okay. Sheriff, that sounds reasonable but I have a few questions and some things to add. First, after discovering the body, Eddie and I went in the cabin. We found the dining room a wreck and someone had left a note on a chair written in Spanish. It said 'You're next'. Eddie took it to mean that he was next."

"Eddie could have written the note." The sheriff interjected.

"He could have." I said, and continued.

I looked over at Frank Reynolds.

"Frank, have you ever been in Eddie's cabin?"

"No. I don't even know where it is."

"What time is it Frank?"

He looked at his watch. "It's 10:20."

"Is that a new watch?" I asked him.

"No. I've had it for years."

"What Eddie doesn't know, is I found a watch in the dining room at the cabin. Eddie was so upset; I stuck it in my jacket pocket and forgot about it. I got to looking at it yesterday and the inside of the band is engraved. It says Frank Reynolds." I held it up for Frank and the sheriff to see.

"You recognize this Frank?" I asked.

"I sure don't. It's not mine."

"I believe you." I said.

"Brian, you did some real estate work for Pioneer Orchards. Did Eddie come see you and request that work to be done?"

"No." He said shaking his head.

"Did he call you and ask for the work to be done?"

"No. I received the request in the mail."

"Did you talk to Eddie or anyone in the family before starting the work?"

"No." He said quickly.

"How did Eddie react when he saw you at the parade yesterday?"

"He let me have it. He called me everything but a white man."

"Is it possible that someone other than Eddie made the request?"

"It's starting to look that way." Brian answered.

"It is common in a crime for someone to be framed. But the strange thing about this case is that several people appear to have been framed. Eddie claims the jar of tainted moonshine was planted in the cabin. Someone left a note in Spanish framing a Hispanic person, perhaps Luis. Someone went to all the trouble to purchase a watch, have it engraved, break it and leave it in the cabin. Someone sent Brian a bunch of topographic maps and instructions for developing part of Pioneer Orchards to make him look like an asshole…Sorry. With all the effort that was put into framing these guys, I am confident that Liliana was murdered. And if I'm right, why? What's the motive? Who has something to gain? Let's go check out the Chevelle. I want to show you something."

We all walked over to the fourth bay and I pulled the cover off the car. Eddie and Skull leaned against the far wall.

"Beautiful car...old...rare.... Really sticks out, wouldn't you say?" I said.

Everyone nodded and agreed.

"If you were going to drive someone out of town, to commit a crime, why would you take a car as unique as this? You wouldn't. But if you wanted to frame the car, how would you do it?"

I punched the garage door opener and as the door rose the sunshine gleamed down on the black paint.

"I'm no Columbo, but late last night I figured it out when my friend Kelly told me she had a flat tire on her vehicle. She evidently hit a curb hard enough to damage the wheel. She said most likely she would need to change the wheel she damaged.

Then it came to me. Eddie's car never made it out to the cabin, only the wheels and tires did. Someone switched wheels with the Chevelle and drove out to the cabin leaving the tread pattern in the driveway. It must have been someone who had access to the shop?"

Everyone became very uncomfortable and began grumbling.

"That's why I asked Kenny Patterson to join us today. Kenny works for GM. Kenny, in your expertise, will these wheels fit on a later model Chevrolet?" "Sure, the bolt pattern is 5 x 4 3/4. That pattern didn't change for decades on certain makes. Virtually any rear wheel drive GM product with a 5 lug pattern will fit. "

"Kenny would these Nova wheels fit on, let's say a four-wheel drive Blazer?"

"No. Not on a four-wheel drive."

"Would they fit on, let's say that 1988 light Blue two-wheel drive Blazer parked right there." I said while pointing at Skull's vehicle.

"Yep." Kenny confirmed.

Everyone turned toward Skull and watched her slowly slide down the wall into a sitting position. Eddie stepped away from her.

19

Skull sobbed and mumbled on and on about how she deserved more and what she was owed and how Eddie was such an asshole. The sheriff and deputy grabbed her by both arms and stood her up. She removed her wedding ring and tossed it in the Chevelle.

"Let's go," she said. "Fuck this place!"

Deputy Myers walked her outside and the sheriff turned toward me.

"Good work, Steve. If you ever want to become a detective, come see me."

Eddie was dumbfounded. "Did that really just happen?" he said.

"I'm afraid so," I said. Are you shocked?"

"I reckon I am. Didn't see that coming. I think the sheriff was ready to haul my ass in."

"She evidently planned it for a long time." I added.

I motioned for everyone to gather around me as if it was story time.

"Here's how I got it figured. Skull and Eddie didn't have the best relationship and she wanted out of it. So she devised a scheme to get rid of Eddie and inherit a big chunk of valuable property at the same time. She must have gone to the courthouse and got information on the various parcels. She made copies of them and gathered topographic maps and mailed them to Brian and asked him to start working on the property development. On Thursday, she knew Eddie called Lily to come clean the shop so she faked receiving a phone message for Eddie and sent him off to Martinsburg just to get him out of town for a few hours. She also knew that was his bowling night so he wouldn't be near the shop for several hours.

Next, she must have met Lily at the shop and took her out to the cabin in her Blazer after she switched the wheels. Remember, Skull used to be a mechanic. She knows her way around the garage. She probably told Lily that they were going to the cabin to clean it instead of the shop.

So, they get up there and she gets Lily to drink some moonshine and eventually poisons her with the jar that she snuck in there that was cut with methanol. They either walked down to the river or maybe Lily ran down there feeling sick. Being poisoned to death must be a miserable way to go. She either hit her head or Skull cracked her upside the noggin after she was already dead. Then Skull pulled her blouse down to reveal her breasts to make it look like a man attacked her.

Next she tears up the cabin, writes the note and purposely leaves the engraved watch behind. Of course she wrote the note in Spanish to throw another wrench into the mystery. She came back to town and switched the wheels back and clean them up."

Luis was shaking his head.

"She was at my house yesterday watching the parade," Frank blurted out.

"I saw her too," Brian chimed in.

"I know. I actually saw her there, too, when Eddie was chewing you out. It puzzled me when Eddie told me she sold her four-wheel drive Blazer and bought an older two wheel drive Blazer. As you know by now, she needed a vehicle that had the same lug nut pattern as the Chevelle."

"What about my Suburban? Did she slash my tires?"

Luis jumped in. "That was those guys with me Friday night. We were pretty sure you killed Liliana. They did it after I went to jail. I will pay you back, man."

"It's okay, Luis. Don't worry about it."

I interrupted them. "Her mistake was framing so many people. I think she thought you guys would fight amongst yourselves and end up killing each other before anyone figured out what actually happened to Lily."

Eddie just shook his head. Luis walked up to Eddie and gave him a hug.

"Eduardo, lo siento me amigo." Luis said.

"I'm sorry too, Luis."

"Please speak English," I requested.

"Oh Eddie, the funeral is Tuesday. You come right?"

"I'll be there, Luis."

Frank, Brian, and Kenny were all looking at me like they were waiting to be excused.

"Thanks guys. You were a big help. I owe you some beers." I said.

"May I have that watch?" Frank asked.

"Okay with me," I said while looking at Eddie. Eddie nodded.

I handed Frank the watch and the three of them walked out slowly while checking out the naked ladies on the old calendars. As they left Art walked in.

"What's all the commotion? Art asked Eddie and me.

"Pop, you won't believe it." Eddie said. "It turns out Linda knocked off Liliana and tried to frame me among some other people. She thought if they put me away, that she would acquire the orchard property. The sheriff just took her away."

"Sorry to hear that, son. She never did seemed satisfied. I have some news too. I skipped church this morning to check out the orchards and we got clobbered last night."

"It was cold last night," I said. Eddie and Art gave me a look.

"How about the old Stayman block. It's on high ground?" Eddie asked.

"Real bad." Art said shaking his head.

"How about the Marshall block?"

"Wiped out. You're mother and I had a talk about an hour ago. And we have decided to throw in the towel."

"Are you serious?" Eddie asked.

"Afraid so. I've had it. Your mother, too. She's more stressed out than I am. Anyway, long story short, we want to shut down the operation. It will take some time to have the paperwork drawn up, but we want to turn everything over to you."

"What will you live on? What will you two do?"

"We're pretty well set financially. Your mother wants to travel. I've had this idea for awhile about starting a business of training hunting dogs. We'll go to flea markets, maybe we'll take up golf."

"I hope you've thought this through Pop." Eddie said.

"We have, son. It's all yours."

Eddie and I watched Art get in his truck where his Dalmatian was waiting impatiently for him to return. We waved as he drove off.

"Well, don't that beat all," Eddie said.

"What?"

"Within a half hour, I lost my wife and inherited a farm."

"Pretty strange." I said. "What do you want to do now, watch the race?"

"They're in Talladega, aren't they? Eddie asked.

"I think so."

Let's go fishing." Eddie yelled.

"Capital idea." I said.

Eddie closed up the garage and threw his gear into the Bronco. We pulled off the lot and immediately began arguing about where to go, what to use, how to fish and what tape to listen to.

"What could Skull have been thinking?" Eddie said, shaking his head.

"She must have lost it," I said.

I told Eddie I enjoyed that Oldies station we listened to yesterday. He adjusted the dial to Oldies 104 just as the song "She's Come Undone" by the Guess Who was winding down. We both sang out loud:

It's too late
She's gone too far
She's lost the sun
She's come undone

Eddie cracked a beer. "No way!" He yelied out loud.

"What?" I asked.

"The funeral. It's Tuesday."

"So?"

"That's Cinco De Mayo."

And that was it.

Made in the USA
Columbia, SC
23 November 2022

71833949R00085